INNOVATIVE TO THE CORE

INNOVATIVE TO THE CORE: STORIES FROM CHINA AND THE WORLD

AUTHORED BY

JUAN ANTONIO FERNANDEZ

China Europe International Business School (CEIBS), China

EMILY M. DAVID

China Europe International Business School (CEIBS), China

AND

SHAOHUI (SOPHIE) CHEN

China Europe International Business School (CEIBS), China

United Kingdom – North America – Japan – India
Malaysia – China

Emerald Publishing Limited
Howard House, Wagon Lane, Bingley BD16 1WA, UK

First edition 2023

British Library Cataloguing in Publication Data
A catalogue record for this book is available from the British Library

ISBN: 978-1-80455-084-7 (Print)
ISBN: 978-1-80455-081-6 ((Online)
ISBN: 978-1-80455-083-0 (Epub)

ISOQAR certified
Management System,
awarded to Emerald
for adherence to
Environmental
standard
ISO 14001:2004.

Certificate Number 1985
ISO 14001

INVESTOR IN PEOPLE

To my wife, Hanning, and my three sons, Simon, Oscar, and Daniel. They are the best that life has given me.

– Juan Antonio

For Diego – my proofreader, support animal, and the love of my life who also happens to be the most innovative person I have ever met. Thank you for doing life with me and making each day more exciting than the one before.

– Emily

To my loving family and friends as my extended family.

– Sophie

CONTENTS

LIST OF FIGURES AND TABLES

Figures

Tables

ABOUT THE AUTHORS

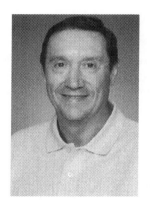

Juan Antonio Fernandez is an Emeritus Professor of Management at China International Business School, Shanghai, China, where he has been a Professor since 2000. He was an Associate Dean and Director of the MBA Program from 2018 to 2020, which ranked two consecutive years fifth worldwide on the *Financial Times* index. He was also the Global EMBA Director from 2012 to 2015. He has taught executive programs in leadership, leading change, and innovation to companies such as Volkswagen, Bank of China, PingAn, IBM, Tencent, Jaguar, Volvo, L'Oréal, and other multinationals. He was a Fellow at Harvard Kennedy School of Government from 2011 to 2012 and again in 2016 and was Visiting Scholar at Lancaster University (UK) in 2006 and 2009.

His prior experience includes serving as the CFO and member of the Board of Directors of Anfi del Mar S.A. (Norway), Advisor to the Ministry of Commerce of the Canary Islands, and financial Analyst for the Industrial Spanish Bank, Spain. He was also the Assistant to the Commercial Attache? of the Spanish Embassy in Venezuela.

He has co-authored seven books, including *China CEO II, China CEO, China Entrepreneur, America Latina en China*, and *China's State-owned Enterprise Reforms*. He has given presentations about his Chinese research in the UK, India, Japan, South Korea, France, Italy, Chile, Peru, Mexico, Mongolia, Ghana, Zambia, and Spain.

He received his PhD and MBA from IESE, Spain. He has a Master of Liberal Arts in Psychology from Harvard University and is currently pursuing a degree in Philosophy from Oxford University.

Emily M. David is an Associate Professor of Organizational Behavior at CEIBS. She earned her PhD in Industrial-Organizational Psychology from the University of Houston and did her undergraduate work at Louisiana State University, earning a perfect 4.0 grade point average. Prior to joining CEIBS, she was an Associate Professor of Management in the College of Business at Zayed University in Dubai, UAE where she served as the Discipline Leader of the HR and Management faculty.

Her current research primarily focuses on discovering how to make workplaces more welcoming for people of all backgrounds and personality profiles in order to achieve better person–organization fit, maximize performance, and avoid employee burnout. She is also interested in fostering helping and other prosocial behaviors in the workplace. Her work has been published in a number of top scholarly outlets such as the *Journal of Management, Journal of Management Studies, Human Relations*, and *Journal of Organizational Behavior*. She was also awarded Poets & Quants prestigious "Best 40 under 40 Business Professors" in 2019.

She is an active member of the Academy of Management and Society for Industrial and Organisational Psychology. She has also worked as an In-house Researcher at both NASA (Wyle Laboratories) and the M.D. Anderson Cancer Centre in addition to consulting for a myriad of organizations including the City of Houston, Kuraray, Saudi ARAMCO, and Exxon Mobil. A true global citizen, she has also traveled extensively through over 42 countries, and has resided in Singapore, China, the UAE, Bolivia, and the USA.

Shaohui (Sophie) Chen is a Professor of Management at CEIBS, where she has been doing case development, teaching, and research work since 2005. She has been serving as the Program Director of Advanced Management Program (a flagship program of Executive Education in CEIBS) and Management Development Program for years. She is also the Core Faculty member of CEIBS Healthcare Sector Research Centre. She had taught at China Institute of Banking and had worked as senior executive for companies in the securities industry for several years.

She received her PhD from The University of Auckland and MS from Renmin University of China. Her research interest has been concentrated on management and employment relations, organizational behavior, leadership, and human resource management. Her research outcomes has been published in academic journals including the *International Journal of Human Resource Management*, the *Asia Pacific Journal of Management*, and *Employee Relations*. She also writes for Chinese business magazines and practitioners. Since 2016, she has initiated a project of Middle-level and First-line Manager Competence Survey and published white papers for three consecutive years.

Her teaching interests focus on organizational management, human resource management and leadership development. Beside teaching for degree programs such as MBA/EMBA and Financial MBA, she has been providing corporate-specific training programs to companies such as China Development Bank, COMAC, Google, CMBC, BCM Leasing, SAICMOTOR, Shanghai Pharma, Tai Ping Life, Sinochem, Eli Lilly, Astrazeneca, Novartis, SANOFI, West China Hospital, Masterkong, Thermo Fisher, Carl Zeiss AG, Huazhu Hotel, etc.

She has been active in providing consulting services and serves as leadership coach and independent director for domestic companies and organizations. She has been the independent member of the Board of Directors of Shengang Securities O. Ltd, the first China-Hong Kong joint venture security company.

ACKNOWLEDGMENTS

We would like to thank, first and foremost, CEIBS for the generous research support that allowed us to undertake this project. We also thank each and every one of our interviewees for sharing the invaluable insights that made this book possible. Finally, we are hugely appreciative of our dedicated agents, Nick Wallwork and Christopher Newson.

1

INTRODUCTION

It is not the strongest of the species which survive nor the most intelligent, but the species most responsive to change.
– Charles Darwin

Today, most companies are on a quest to become more innovative. By that, they often mean going digital, selling their products online, updating their website, or creating a mobile App. Although all of these are great initiatives, we believe that true innovation runs deeper than these surface-level interventions. To quote the old saying of "putting lipstick on a pig," such efforts in isolation often mean that the exterior changes but the core remains the same. This book is about helping cultures to become innovative to their core, so that innovation becomes the default way of doing things rather than a one-time cosmetic change.

Innovation, like leadership, is something that people can easily identify but often have more trouble defining. In informal discussions, it is frequently used interchangeably with words like creativity and invention. However, there are crucial differences between these overlapping concepts. Creativity is simply the generation of new ideas. Some of these ideas might become new products and services, but many will either die or accumulate dust in a forgotten location. Inventions, by contrast, are the creation of a new product usually in a lab or a research center. Many inventions become patents that can be incorporated into future products. Often, inventions take time to mature and evolve until they become a viable product.

Although innovation incorporates creativity and invention, these two factors alone are not sufficient for innovation to occur. We define innovation as a change in a product, a service, or business model that helps to drive profits or gain market share. The willingness of consumers to pay for the new product or service is the key defining factor that distinguishes innovation from creative ideas and new inventions. Kenneth Yu, the former President of 3M Greater China Area, eloquently described innovation in the following way.

> *First and foremost, innovation is an art. It is not a science, although because of innovation, a lot of scientific new things can be introduced. But the concept of innovation by itself is not a science. You cannot say that if the company follows these steps the company or the person will become innovative. It doesn't work that way. You need a culture that has to be developed over time.*

This perspective captures the fact that, while easy to understand conceptually, innovation is often quite difficult to introduce in practice. To effectively bring innovation to the core, there are no shortcuts or one-step solutions. Instead, organizations need to be nurtured and reinforced through multi-faceted efforts to change the leadership practices, systems, and employee behaviors. Each of these factors alone is insufficient to induce innovation to the core. Consistent messages from all three components are needed to produce deeply ingrained innovation so it becomes the way of doing things in the organization. Kenneth from 3M shared with us that sometimes innovative products may seem like failures until their time comes. New ideas might be born ahead of their time but should not be forgotten; someday they might find their market.

INNOVATION STORIES

An Invention Ahead of Its Time at 3M by Kenneth Yu

Someone invented a way to recycle light. You know, light goes in all directions. We developed at 3M a film that reflected the light back so that the light is not wasted. This resulted in a light bulb that consumed only a small fraction of the normal energy needed. But how many bulbs can you sell? Besides, the margin is very small. In a way, it was a marginal invention for 3M. Years later, the world saw all the new products like notebook computers, cell phones, iPads, digital TVs, etc. If you use your cell phone, you care about battery life. The amount of power in your battery is limited, so the solution was to have bigger batteries. Our customers came to us with this challenge – how can we reduce the energy consumption so that we can have smaller batteries and reduce the size of those gadgets?

The highest consumption of energy comes from the screen. Somebody at 3M remembered the film that reflected the light back and forth and they tested it. It worked very well; the screen looks just as bright with less energy consumed, therefore leading to longer battery life. The film was able to recycle about 90% of the light coming out from the light source. A high-definition TV consumes more power, and all the components are much hotter as the light increases. You must make a large light enhancement film to use less power. As an example of incremental improvement, the film didn't just enhance the light, it also enhanced the sharpness of the image. And the rest is history. Until today, as we are talking, 3M still owns a lion's share of many of the large panel TVs.

In the story above, Kenneth provides an example of an invention that ultimately revolutionized the industry but took years to become an innovation. The film was invented about two decades before 3M was able to monetize it. Kenneth added:

> *Commercialization is just like this. 3M made a lot of money with this film. The customer is also happy because now the cell phones and the notebooks can work for a much longer amount of time. This is an example of an invention that became a great success years after it was created.*

This highlights the importance of company memory, so inventions are not forgotten when their time comes.

Often when people think about innovation, they mistakenly assume that it must be something completely novel that disrupts the old ways. As an example of disruptive innovation, Kenneth from 3M points to Thomas Edison's invention of the light bulb, which transformed the way people live. In contrast, modern innovations are often incremental improvements or old technology implemented in new contexts. As a key example of this distinction, Kenneth pointed to the Chinese giant, Alibaba:

> *Alibaba certainly did not invent the cell phone. They did not invent the QR code. They invented Alipay. Likewise, Tencent invented WeChat Pay, which is a new way of payment. But they were not the first companies that did this. Hong Kong had previously been using the Octopus Card,*

for example. But somehow, they came up with Alipay using existing technologies and took advantage of the fact that everyone has a cell phone [to innovate payment transactions in China].

True innovation occurs when people have a vision for a better product or way of doing things and they can translate this idea into commercial value. To foster these types of ideas in countries and organizations, you must become innovative to the core. 3M is an excellent example of a company that has embedded innovation at all levels of the organization. The story of how Post-it notes were created by accident is very well known; what began as a failure to create a strong aircraft adhesive ultimately resulted in 3M's signature product. What is not so well known is how Post-it notes were initially commercialized.

INNOVATION STORIES

How 3M's Post-it Notes Went Viral by Kenneth Yu

I was with 3M when the Post-it note was first invented. I can tell you a story now. This might be the first time you hear this. I got this from the person who championed the project. He lives in San Antonio and is a good friend of mine, Dr Geoffrey Nicholson. But he's not the only hero of this story. You may have heard the story about that the choir that used it as a paper marker. That is true. But that did not sell the product. We did not formally market or commercialize the product. In those days, they weren't called Post-it notes, we just called them sticky notes. Dr Nicholson noticed that the department secretaries at 3M really liked them. He talked to our CEO and asked him to send a box of sticky notes to other 500 CEOs of top companies in the USA. Our CEO asked those other CEOs to give the product to their secretaries to see if they like it.

If you are the CEO of Boeing, and you get a letter from the CEO of 3M, you do not throw it away. So, they gave the sticky notes to their secretaries and did not think too much about it after that. The secretaries started using these sticky notes on memos that they would send to the boss for signature and to other departments. Very quickly, the sticky notes propagated in the organization from the top down. So, the secretaries went to their bosses and asked for more sticky notes. They sent the request back to 3M CEO. Our CEO asked Nicholson to take care of it. We then stopped giving them away and commercialized them. We came up with a name, the packaging, and everything. You can imagine that each of the 500 secretaries could easily influence at least 10 others, so it went viral. Fluid communication inside the organization is key for innovation.

In sum, creativity is the generation of ideas. Some of these ideas become inventions, and creative outputs become innovations when they find a market (Fig. 1.1). To enhance the chances of this happening, we echo the sage advice of the two-time Nobel prize winner in physics, Linus Pauling, who once said, "The best way to have a good idea is to have a lot of ideas."

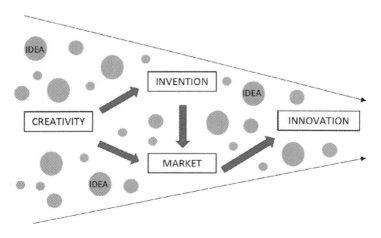

Source: Authors' original work.

Fig. 1.1. The Funnel Model of Innovation.

WHY WE WROTE THIS BOOK

Scholars and practitioners agree that innovation is perhaps more of a business imperative today than at any other point in history. When serving a world that is increasingly more volatile, uncertain, complex, and ambiguous (VUCA), countries and businesses must be able to agilely respond to changing environmental circumstances and consumer preferences.[1] Thriving in such a world requires leaders that can act on input from all levels, who design systems that reinforce innovative priorities, and who can anticipate the changing needs of its citizens and consumers. Continuous learning should take place and norms of open and informal communication should be encouraged. As we are currently living and working at the intersection of globalization, digitization, and a global COVID-19 pandemic, the time is ripe to further explore how innovative cultures at all levels can be built and reinforced.

Although much has been written on the topic of innovation, as business professors based in China, we saw a unique opportunity for a book that consolidates the lessons that China and the World can learn from each other. To this end, we aimed to better understand the core components of established innovative companies around the world in the hopes that firms can adopt some of these best practices as they continue their rapid progression from an innovation adopter to and innovation generators.

WHO IS IN THIS BOOK?

To build on the quantitative insights provided by our survey, we conducted 30 in-depth interviews with subject matter experts. To achieve a balanced perspective, we focused on gaining wisdom from top managers and consultants hailing from around the world. We focused on talking to seasoned business leaders who were either raised or had worked in some of the most innovative countries in the world and those who worked for some of the most innovative companies in the world. These included executives at multinational organizations, entrepreneurs, consultants, and people working for governments and in nonprofit innovation centers. In Tables 1.1 and 1.2, we provide a snapshot of the interviewees you will hear from over the course of this book.

Table 1.1. Experts and Consultants (In Alphabetic Order).

	Name	Nationality	Company	Position	Country	Website
1	Cameron Johnson	USA	Tidalwave Solutions	Partner	China	www.tidalwave.com
2	Daniel Wang	China	CEIBS eLab	Director	China	www.ceibs.edu
3	Hellmut Schutte	Germany	Former Dean Instead Singapore	Professor at INSEAD	France	www.insead.edu
4	Jari Grosse-Ruyken	Germany	hivetime	Managing Partner	China	www.hivetime.com
5	Jonathan Woetzel	USA	McKinsey & Company	Senior Partner, Director Global Institute	Global	www.mckinesy.com
6	Martin Bech	Denmark	Academy of Technical Sciences (ATV)	Advisor	Denmark	www.atv.dk
7	Nicolas Musy	Switzerland	The Swiss Centers	Founder	China	www.swisscenters.org
8	Omar Al-Busaidy	UAE	UAE Consulate in New York	Economic Affairs	Dubai	u.ae
9	Ramon Baeza	Spain	BGC	MG & Senior Partner	USA	www.bcg.com
10	Roy Chason	Israel	KnoHao	Founder	Spain	www.kno-hao.com
11	Tae-Yeol Kim	South Korea	Professor of Management	CEIBS	China	www.ceibs.edu

Source: Authors' original work.

Table 1.2. Company Executives (In Alphabetic Order).

	Name	Nationality	Company	Position	Country	Website
1	Changjun Sun	China	TUV Rheinland, China	Consultant	Germany	www.tuv.com/greater-china/en/
2	Congwei (Eric) Huang	China	Shanghai Zaitu Network Technology	Founder	China	www.z-trip.cn/
3	David Ferreira	South Africa	Discovery Limited	General Manager for China, Discovery Group	South Africa	www.discovery.co.za
4	David Wang	China	Buhler	President China	Switzerland	www.bhuler.com
5	Hang (Shawn) Cheng	China	HUPU	Founder	China	www.hupu.com
6	Huijie Hong	China	MITS (Shanghai) Technology	Founder	China	
7	Jason Yin	China	Kimberly-Clark, China	CFO	China	www.kimberly-clark.com/en-us/
8	Jerry Liu	China	Cargill	President China	USA	www.cargill.com
9	Jun Wang	China	Oerlikon Management AG	Country President, China	Switzerland	www.oerlikon.com/en/
10	Kamal Dhuper	India	NIIT	CEO China	India & USA	www.niit.com

(Continued)

Table 1.2. (Continued)

	Name	Nationality	Company	Position	Country	Website
11	Kenneth Yu	Hong Kong, China	3M, China	Former President 3M Greater China	USA	www.3m.com
12	Kern Peng	Hong Kong, China	INTEL	Laboratory Head	USA	www.intel.com
13	MatsHarborn	Sweden	Scania	President, China	Sweden	www.scania.com
14	Xiaolin Yuan	China	Volvo Car	President & CEO Asia Pacific	China	www.volvocars.com
15	Yang Bing	China	DEWU	Founder & President	China	www.dewu.com
16	Zhenping (Ben) Zheng	China	Openex Intelligent Technology	CEO & Founder	China	www.openex-int.com/
17	Zhifeng (Forrester) Zhang	China	Hotelbeds Shanghai	Director, GM	China	www.hotelbeds.com/home

Source: Authors' original work.

In total, this book incorporates the combined experience of more than 30 experts and top executives (some of whom wished to remain anonymous) with the 40+ years of cumulative experience of the three authors, who are Organizational Behavior and Leadership Professors at China Europe International Business School (www.ceibs.edu).

STRUCTURE OF THE BOOK

We aimed to present two primary categories of insights on innovation: one on a more macro-level featuring the determinants of innovative countries, and the another on a more micro-level showcasing the components of innovative organizational cultures. As a result, we organized the book into these two sections. Sections I and II are independent of each other. Readers can choose to start at the one that interests them the most.

For Section I, we first looked to recent innovation reports to help us narrow down our countries of interest. These were: (1) INSEAD's Global Innovation Index 2021, (2) the World Economic Forum's Global Competitiveness Report 2019, and (3) IMD's World Digital Competitiveness Ranking 2021. By triangulating these sources, we chose the following countries:

- *Large countries*: United States of America (USA) and China.

- *Small and middle-sized countries*: Switzerland, Sweden, Denmark, South Korea, and Israel.

- *Young countries*: Singapore and the United Arab Emirates (UAE).

This selection represents not only some of the most innovative countries in the world, but also reflects a wide variety of sizes and geographical locations. Although there are many other very innovative countries, we decided to focus on these few in the interest of parsimony. The idea is to explore innovation occurring in countries with different historical and cultural backgrounds that are also located in different parts of the world. We will explore their history, culture, and the role of the government in innovation.

We believe that country-level innovation can often serve as a key determinant of innovation at the micro-level, which is the focus of Section II: innovation at company level.

For Section II, the first step we took when researching this book was to conduct our own large-scale innovation survey. In the Fall of 2020, 950 executives responded to our questionnaire, 72% of which were male and 96% of whom had more than 10 years of work experience. We gained many interesting insights from the survey responses, which we compiled into the 2021 CEIBS Innovation Survey Report.[2] For instance, we found that participants working in the technology, healthcare, and services sectors reported the highest levels of innovation whereas those working in the financial, real estate, and energy industries reported the lowest levels of innovation. In addition, we found that executives reporting high levels of innovation in their firms were significantly more likely to see the value of innovation and were also much less likely to want to leave their jobs. To fuel innovative cultures, 55% of respondents reported that continuous experimentation was the most important driver, whereas 52% selected quickly responding to customer needs, and 35% believed clear communication of the organization's values and principles was most critical. In terms of current organizational practices, 70% of respondents reported that their firm introduced new products or services in the last three years whereas only 21% reported that they had purchased advanced machinery or new technology. Finally, we found that innovative cultures are composed of three critical components: (a) leader words and behaviors, (b) agile organizational policies and practices, and (c) collaborative and experimental employee norms.

We used the components of innovative cultures identified by our survey – organizational policies, leadership, and talent – to dictate the content of Section II. We then augmented these sections by conducting interviews with the innovation experts and top executives that were highlighted previously. Finally, we also incorporated the BCG ranking of the world's Most Innovative Companies 2021 and other public sources to identify key target companies such as 3M and Intel. According to this report, there is clear evidence that innovation is a driver of value, with the 50 most innovative companies on their list beating the MSCI world by more than 3% in total shareholder return per year between 2005 and 2020. They also highlight the increased representation of Chinese companies on the list since 2005, underscoring the importance of understanding the innovation occurring in this region. Finally, they found that only three quarters of surveyed companies are committed to innovation, highlighting an important opportunity for the remaining organizations who wish to undergo this critical cultural transformation.

We created a framework to illustrate the necessary conditions for taking innovation to the core of the organization (Fig. 1.2). We will explore these different components in depth in Section II of the book.

Many companies are facing the need to innovate to survive. This book is for those business leaders that want innovation to become the default mode in their organization and a cornerstone of their company culture. We sincerely hope you find the ideas outlined in our book helpful in your quest to make your company innovative to the core.

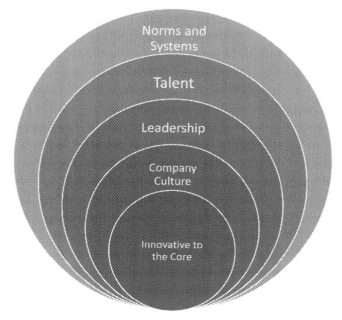

Source: Authors' original work.

Fig. 1.2.   Innovation to the Core.

NOTES

1. Millar, C. C. J. M., Groth, O., & Mahon, J. F. (2018). Management innovation in a VUCA world: Challenges and recommendations. *California Management Review, 61*(1), 5–14.

2. https://www.ceibs.edu/sites/ceibs.sit.site1.drupalagile.com/files/import_files/sites/default/files/research/reports/others/2021-innovation-survey-report-en.pdf

Section I

INNOVATION AT THE COUNTRY LEVEL

In the first section of this book, we adopted a macro lens to analyze what makes entire countries and peoples innovative. Our goals were twofold: to understand (a) what makes some countries more innovative than others and (b) what other economies can learn from them. To this end, we sought out interviewees with knowledge about a diverse range of innovative countries of all sizes and spread across geographical locations around the world. To identify our target countries, we used a triangulation method based on three international surveys: (1) INSEAD's Global Innovation Index 2021, (2) the World Economic Forum's Global Competitiveness Report 2019,[1] and (3) IMD's World Digital Competitiveness Ranking 2021 (Fig. I.1).

Using the ranking of the three surveys, we selected the following countries:

- *Large countries*: USA and China.

- *Small and middle-sized countries*: Switzerland, Sweden, Denmark, South Korea, and Israel.

- *Young countries*: Singapore and the UAE.

As you can see in Table I.1, these countries consistently rank among the most innovative countries in the world across the three reports.

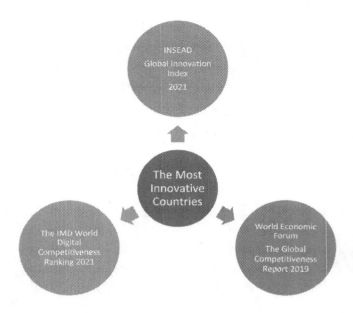

Source: Authors' original work.

Fig. I.1.   Most Innovative Country Sources.

Our investigation serves as a timely update of Michael Porter's 1990 *Harvard Business Review* article, "The Competitive Advantage of Nations." In this article, he sagely argues that national prosperity is deliberately created rather than passively inherited because of natural resources or strong economies and currencies. At the heart of a country's prosperity, Porter argues, is a strong tradition of innovation – both in terms of new technologies and new ways of doing business. Strong internal competition, an ample local supplier network, and demanding local consumers are the factors that fuel this innovation. Often, countries will choose to specialize in a small number of key industries in which they carve out their competitive advantage. As examples, he highlights German cars and chemicals, Japanese semi-conductors, Swiss banking and pharmaceuticals, and the US's aircraft and movie industries.

Although many of his insights on country and organizational innovation remain true today, there are several reasons why an updated treatment of this topic is warranted. Below, we highlight

Table I.1. Country Rankings by International Innovation Reports.

	INSEAD Global Innovation Index 2021	WEF Global Competitiveness Report 2019	IMD World Digital Competitiveness Ranking 2020
1	Switzerland	Singapore	USA
2	Sweden	USA	Singapore
3	USA	Hong Kong (China)	Denmark
4	UK	Netherlands	Sweden
5	Republic of Korea	Switzerland	Hong Kong (China)
6	Netherlands	Japan	Switzerland
7	Finland	Germany	Netherlands
8	Singapore	Sweden	Republic of Korea
9	Denmark	UK	Norway
10	Germany	Denmark	Finland
Rank	China – 12	Republic of Korea – 13	UAE – 14
	Israel – 15	Israel – 20	China – 16
	UAE – 33	UAE – 25	Germany – 18
		China – 28	Israel – 19

Sources: https://www.imd.org/centers/world-competitiveness-center/rankings/world-digital-competitiveness/; https://www3.weforum.org/docs/WEF_TheGlobalCompetitivenessReport2019.pdf; https://www.insead.edu/newsroom/2021-global-innovation-index-2021-innovation-investments-resilient-despite-covid-19-pandemic

the three biggest shifts that have occurred over the last 30 years that have had a clear and disruptive impact on innovation and business practices:

1. Globalization has accelerated, giving small nations access to world markets. Large domestic markets are no longer necessary to become an innovation superpower. This trend is most evident when examining the rise of countries like Singapore, the UAE, Israel, Switzerland, Sweden, and Denmark. Indeed, studies have noted that international trade has increased exponentially in the last century, with the value of global exports more than tripling over the last three decades.[2] According to the World Bank, globalization and stronger open trade policies have dramatically increased innovation and economic growth for all.[3]

2. Digitalization has changed the dynamic of business in the world. A recent report by the European Commission[4] has demonstrated that this trend has fundamentally changed the way businesses communicate, the platforms they work on, their sales and marketing strategies (e.g., social media and e-commerce), and the types of solutions and products they offer. As a result of digitalization, we now see increased competition in industries that were viewed as impenetrable 30 years ago, including car manufacturing, logistics, and finance. In addition, countries like China have leveraged the digital economy to attain a meteoric rise in innovation rankings, most recently moving up 15 spots in the 2021 IMD report on Digital Competitiveness[5] to #15. Notably, the USA, Singapore, Switzerland, the UAE, and the Scandinavian Countries all scored highly on this ranking as well.

3. Perhaps the biggest change in the global business landscape has been the emergence of China as a key world player. At the time of Porter's article, China was a poor country. Today, it is on track to become the largest economy in the world. As noted by a recent McKinsey report on The China Effect on Global Innovation,[6] China has imparted its own brand of innovation on the world, displaying a unique model of customer-focused and iterative innovation that capitalizes on its large and dynamic market. This model, they argue, is likely to prove disruptive on the global stage, helping to meet unmet needs in goods and services in both emerging markets and advanced economies.

To glean updated insights into what makes some countries and economies more innovative than others, we used in-depth interviews with experts from different nations and with experience working in various locations around the globe.

STRUCTURE OF THE CHAPTERS IN SECTION I

To organize our country insights, we use three chapters (Fig. I.2). The first focuses on the innovation factors that have given rise to the most innovative countries around the world. These include historical events, cultural factors, educational policies, national safety,

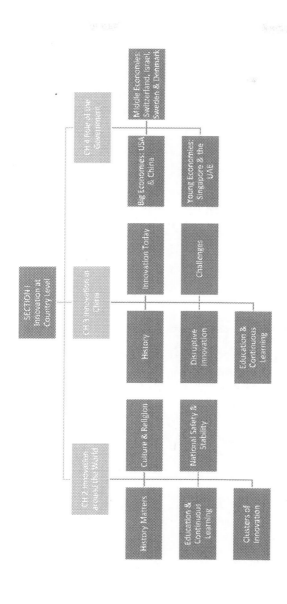

Source: Authors' original work.

Fig. I.2.   Section I Structure.

and clustering. Next, we do a deep dive into Chinese innovation. As a relatively new player in this arena, we note the unique influences that have led to China's unique brand of innovation. These include historical factors, education, and consumer attitudes toward innovation. We conclude this chapter by outlining potential challenges that may lay ahead as China continues to move from being an innovation absorber to an innovation leader. Finally, we devote a chapter to analyzing the diverse roles that governments can play in supporting and driving innovation.

NOTES

1. The WEF published a special report in 2020 on the impact of COVID-19, so we opted to use the 2019 report instead.

2. Federico, G., & Tena-Junguito, A. (2016). *A tale of two globalizations: Gains from trade and openness 1800–2010.* CEPR WP.11128, Centre for Economic Policy Research, London.

3. https://www.worldbank.org/en/results/2018/04/03/stronger-open-trade-policies-enables-economic-growth-for-all

4. https://op.europa.eu/en/publication-detail/-/publication/203fa0ec-e742-11ea-ad25-01aa75ed71a1/language-en

5. https://www.imd.org/centers/world-competitiveness-center/rankings/world-digital-competitiveness/

6. https://www.mckinsey.com/~/media/McKinsey/Featured%20Insights/Innovation/Gauging%20the%20strength%20of%20Chinese%20innovation/MGI%20China%20Effect_Executive%20summary_October_2015.ashx

2

INNOVATION AROUND THE WORLD

I have worked for seven years in the US, and I admire the US people. China still has a long way to catch up in terms of tolerating failure, and that's something I think is bigger in the US than in Europe. In the US if you fail, then you try again. That is very important.

– Jerry Liu, President of Cargill China

INTRODUCTION

Over the course of our research and interviews, it became apparent that there were certain localized determinants of innovation. Interviewees frequently cited historical, geographical, and cultural elements that drove innovation both in the past and today. The importance of these ingrained factors is illustrated by the remarkable year-on-year stability of the most innovative countries in the world according to INSEAD's Global Innovation Index (GII). For example, Switzerland, Sweden, the United States (USA), Germany, and Singapore have been consistent members of the top 10 in every year that the survey has been conducted. Israel, Denmark, and the United Arab Emirates (UAE) have made notable upward moves in the last few years, ranking #15, #9, and #33 in the 2021 ranking. The primary formula for becoming a champion of INSEAD's GII is to have an open economy and high standards for education. Although spending on human capital is the best investment you can make – the report notes that the highest-quality universities are in the USA, United Kingdom (UK), and China, respectively – having an open economy is a big part of the reason why there are several small countries that consistently rank among the most innovative, including Singapore, Switzerland, and the Scandinavian countries.

In this chapter, we will describe the primary factors that led to innovation of certain countries and peoples. To this end, we will explore the role of history, geographical factors, natural resources, religion, and culture in fostering innovation. To illustrate the potency of these factors, we will explore detailed examples of some of the world's most innovative countries in North America, Europe, the Middle East, and Asia.

HISTORY AND ENVIRONMENT

One consistent theme that arose when speaking to people around the world about innovation was the importance of a pivotal event or decision point in history. Often spurred by major global events, such as wars, or the forward-thinking vision of the country's leaders, interviewees pointed to several pivotal moments from the past that put their countries on a path toward innovation. Sometimes, this decision point was spurred by factors inherent in their localized environment, such as a lack of natural resources or increasing threat and competition from neighboring nations. For others, it was the type of people who were attracted to settle the land and the cultural artifacts that this created. In this section, we highlight each of these historical factors that helped to set the stage for innovation in some of the world's most inventive countries.

The USA serves as a prime example of an innovation superpower whose culture has been extensively shaped by historical factors. For one, the USA is a relatively young country that is fundamentally a nation of immigrants. It is important to note, however, that immigration is a necessary, but not a sufficient, condition for innovation. For example, other nations like Argentina also have a rich history of immigration but have not made notable advancements in the innovation sector. In contrast with other European and Asian cultures that had centuries to solidify their cultures with little to no international input, Americans had to learn to assimilate diverse ideas and learn how to communicate across cultures from the country's very inception. This led to several cultural attributes that helped to foster innovation. For one, whereas other cultures, such as Japan, had many years to develop indirect ways of reading between the lines when communicating, Americans hailing from various parts of the globe had to be as direct as possible when communicating to ensure that they were being understood.[1]

The fact that the USA was initially populated by people fleeing more established countries and societies in pursuit of greater freedom, opportunity, or adventure, has also greatly shaped American culture. Just as early pilgrims were lured by possibility, the so-called "American Dream" continued to evolve as people left the early cities to seek fortune in the Wild West. When the direct and informal nature of communicating was combined with this inherent appetite for risk-taking, the resulting culture is one where the prospect of becoming a "self-made success" outweighs the potential embarrassment of failure along the way. This is something that Jerry Liu, a Chinese national who got an MBA at Wharton and is now the President of Cargill China, admires. As noted in the opening quote for this chapter, he sees America's tolerance of failure to be a key driver of innovation. His insights are particularly valuable given that innovation is ingrained within Cargill's core mission. Despite the passing of years, Cargill has remained true to the original vision of its founder, W. W. Cargill: helping farmers prosper, connecting markets, and bringing consumers the products they're seeking. Along the way, it has fundamentally advanced how the food and agriculture industry work. Cargill's core goal is to use innovation as a tool to sustainably nourish the world well into the future. Cargill's innovation centers in Europe, North America, and Asia, including China, enable it stay at the forefront of emerging customer needs and solutions. To build awareness of the novel offerings they are producing, it holds a "Product Innovation Day" every year to display their new R&D products and formulas.[2]

Cameron Johnson,[3] an American partner at Tidalwave Solutions, a consulting company located in Shanghai, reiterates the importance of risk-taking and accepting mistakes for the process of innovation. He contends that tales of Americans risking it all have become glorified and entrenched in local folklore, and cited several famous examples:

> There is the famous Edison line of "I didn't fail 1,000 times. The light bulb was an invention with 1,000 steps." … Steve Jobs started Apple in his garage and ended up becoming one of the richest people in the world. Jeff Bezos started out literally sitting in a tiny office in Seattle, selling books on a website nobody ever heard of and is now the richest man in the world. These are all stories of people who put all of their cards on the table, pushed their chips to the center, and really pushed forward.

The ability to attract and retain the best and brightest minds from around the world is another thing that the USA has traditionally excelled at. Even today, there continues to be an influx of workers immigrating to the USA to build new companies and fuel innovation. Modern examples include Elon Musk (the founder of Tesla) from South Africa and Sergey Brin (the founder of Google) from Russia. As we will elaborate more on later, part of the attraction is the high-quality universities in the USA. For example, Sundar Pichai (the CEO of Google) initially immigrated to the USA to attend Stanford University in 1993. Cameron from Tidlewave agrees that this immigrant DNA continues to contribute to innovation today, though things have been complicated by modern politics. He said that:

> In the US, you really can come from anywhere and develop a business and be rewarded for it. This really is not the case, I would argue, in many other countries. Where I grew up in Seattle, you were always surrounded by people who were from somewhere else, whether they were immigrants or children of immigrants. That's part of the culture and it's absolutely a benefit. The greatest city in the world is New York City. Why? Because every culture, language, and ethnicity lives within the city's borders.

A second historical reason is that up until very recently, it was rather difficult to get adequate funding for entrepreneurial ventures in most countries. Even today, the USA has the largest and most efficient liquid capital market in the world.[4] This fuels innovation in two ways: (1) by attracting would-be entrepreneurs to come to the USA from other places and (2) by incentivizing people to innovate in order to be rewarded by the capital market. In some cases, this can even create a self-sustaining loop of exponential innovation. Jerry from Cargill cites Tesla as an example of this localized factor:

> Elon Musk started PayPal and got the money to do the other ventures. Today the capital market is the biggest supporter of Tesla and I think the capitalization of Tesla may be even more than GM. That's a game changer. No other country offers these types of opportunities.

He contrasts the capital situation in the USA with China and Europe, where most of the R&D is funded by the government rather than the capital market. Cameron from Tidlewave also suggested that the prospect of an initial public offering (IPO) is something that helps to reward good products, even if they are unrelated to one another. Citing the example of Elon Musk again, he notes that the Tesla founder is famous for

> *producing good products in multiple industries. He started with the car, then the solar panels, and now he's doing SpaceX. These are areas where he's also become a bit of a celebrity. And that doesn't happen in most places in the world.*

In sum, historical factors in the USA have fostered a culture of risk-taking, a tolerance of failure, a diverse talent pool from around the world, and a capital market that allows people to profit from their ideas, regardless of how varied they are. This has led to a surplus of innovative technologies and industries, with the USA having a pioneering and leading role in the semiconductor, software, aerospace, healthcare, and traditional finance industries.

Many innovative countries, however, are much smaller in size and boast much fewer human capital and natural resources than places like China and the USA. One example of a country that has shot to the forefront of the world stage in terms of innovation is the UAE. According to Omar Al-Busaidy, an Emirati Fulbright Scholar and employee in the Ministry of Foreign Affairs and International Cooperation at the UAE Consulate in New York, his country's reputation as an innovation leader began with the decline of the pearling industry in the UAE in the late 1920s and early 1930s. Although the industry created a period of wealth for the country starting in the mid-1800s, by the early twentieth century this industry began plummeting. This crash was precipitated by both the Great Depression and innovations by the Japanese, who learned how to make flawless artificial pearls. The decimation of Dubai's primary industry also happened before oil was discovered and before the disjointed emirates joined together in 1971 as the single country that is now known as the UAE. Thus, the leaders of the individual emirates learned an early lesson to avoid relying too much on any one resource. As Omar summarized, *the question became for Dubai, what will happen when we deplete whatever resource that we currently depend on? How can we move forward? How can we innovate and how can we grow our economy?*

For the UAE, the answer to these questions was to invest any current resources into creating a sustainable, resilient, and diverse economic base. As Omar notes:

The next resource we had – which we knew from Day 1 was limited in Dubai – was oil. We said, let's bank as much as we can and leverage this resource that we have and use this money to fund the sectors of the economy that will be crucial for the future of the country. And that's the reason why the UAE has always had this forward-thinking strategy, particularly with innovation.

With this forward-thinking vision in place, the previous ruler of Dubai – Sheikh Rashid Al Maktoum – undertook two major projects. The first was to build an international port and the second was to build the Dubai Creek, which is an artificial creek. To fund these projects, they borrowed money from the government of Kuwait. These early advancements helped to significantly increase trade between the UAE and both India and Iran.

INNOVATION STORIES

Jacque Cousteau's Discovery of Oil in Abu Dhabi by Omar Al-Busaidy

There are a lot of stories of how certain foreign individuals contributed significantly to the development of the country over the course of its history. I always like to ask people: "How do you think the UAE discovered oil?" Actually, all the big oil companies said that Abu Dhabi did not have any oil. Imagine! Oil was first discovered in Bahrain in the Gulf and then in Saudi Arabia. Afterwards, all these big companies came to Abu Dhabi, but they couldn't find oil and they all left. Then came Jacques Cousteau, the marine biologist, and his very famous boat named Calypso. Jacques Cousteau took Sheikh Shakhbut's boat, who was Sheikh Zayed's (the founder of the UAE) brother and the ruler of Abu Dhabi at the time. Jacques Cousteau knew there was oil here because he was marine biologist. Even today, when you go to Abu Dhabi National Oil Company's headquarters, the first thing any guest sees is a video of Sheikh Shakbut and Jacques Cousteau. We found oil because of Jacques Cousteau.

Never content with the status quo, the rulers of the UAE set their sights on becoming the best transportation and logistics hub in the world. In our conversation, Omar shared the vision and motivation behind this goal. He said:

> *Sheikh Mohammed Bin Rashed Al Maktoum, the Ruler of Dubai and Vice President of the UAE, has frequently said that for any country to succeed, you have to invest in two main sectors: infrastructure and security.*

His definition of infrastructure includes both soft infrastructure – which involves ample investments in education – and hard infrastructure – which led Sheikh Mohammed to invest in the highest-quality roads, bridges, seaports, and airports. By setting up this world-class infrastructure, Dubai's goal was to become a base or a stopover in the Middle East for Western companies hoping to get their products and services to the Eastern Hemisphere. Fast-forward to today, and Dubai now runs the third largest re-export hub in the world after Hong Kong and Singapore.

They also replicated this ocean-based success in the air. The world-famous Emirates Airlines started with the Dubai government borrowing two second-hand planes from Pakistan. Their first innovation in their sector was expanding their sights beyond simply moving people to moving goods. Today, Emirates Airlines is not only one of the biggest and most successful passenger aircrafts, but also one of the best cargo air carriers in the world.

INNOVATION STORIES

How the UAE Created One of the Most
Successful Airline Companies in the World by
Omar Al-Busaidy

Emirates Airlines asked themselves how can we be different from the rest of the airlines? Before, only three carriers were consistently making headlines: Cathay Pacific, Singapore Airlines, and Thai Air. What do these three companies have in common? The same kind of culture: Asian hospitality. You notice immediately when you go into Asian hotels and resorts, they're super hospitable. Emirates Airlines asked themselves, "how can we offer that same level of hospitality combined with Western quality standards?" They then brought in all these different minds to create this perfect mix.

When you look at the Emirates crews today – they're so diverse. The whole team is very diverse; it's not just like all Asian, all Arab, or any one group. But also, no aircraft on their fleet is older than five years old. That's the reason the planes are very clean and why they are very good. Other airlines usually keep their planes for 10 years. This begs the question of what we do with all those older aircrafts. In another example of innovation, Emirates Airlines decided to lease them to other countries in Africa, Asia, and some parts of Europe that almost never purchase brand-new aircrafts. Their priority is to move people. Our priority is to let people have a great experience in the air. That strategy allowed the UAE to be a step ahead of the rest of the competition because we always have had new planes.

I remember the two British executives who started the airline. They started with only two airplanes and fifty million dollars. They spoke to Sheikh Mohammed and explained the strategy for the airline. The second most important thing they asked was to invest quickly in the airport, because the airport is the first and the last impression of every country. How do you make the airport appealing and attractive? Duty free was the answer. And that's why our airport is super

successful. Another reason is that they have a lot of fran-
chises and control the permits to be able to bring in certain
goods and resources into the UAE. Even if you don't have a
resource, you can still control it. We can sell so many different products because Emirates owns the rights for the whole
MENA region. That's how we have the funds for Emirates.
Western airlines wonder how in the world is Emirates able
to fuel its planes at the rate that they are? They're paying so
much for fuel. Well, we're paying the same price, but we have
other sources of revenue to compensate for the cost of fuel.
And that's why flights are so cheap on Emirates if you buy a
plane ticket from outside the country.

Despite these rapid and notable achievements in infrastructure,
the Dubai government once again moved the goalpost for themselves. Intent on becoming a sustainable and knowledge-based
economy, they innovated yet again by translating their success in
running the port into the creation of Dubai Ports World. Rather
than being content to control such a powerful part of world trade,
they sold the secrets of their success as a knowledge-based com-
modity. As Omar shared with us,

> we started to make purchases and agreements with
> other countries around the world to operate their ports.
> In fact, almost 40% of the goods in every household
> in the world have either gone through Dubai or gone
> through a port that's managed and operated by Dubai
> Ports World.

By owning or operating ports in Africa, South America, the USA,
Europe, and Asia, they were also able to expand their diplomatic
influence on the world at large.

Denmark is another country that has managed to become a
leader in innovation despite having very few resources. For example, it has a very small population of roughly 5.8 million people in
2020.[5] There are no major mountains, rivers, forests, or minerals to
be mined. According to Martin Bech, the Danish national Advisor
at the Danish Academy of Technical Science, this scarcity creates an

impetus to think outside the box and find new ways of succeeding as a nation. It also fuels innovation to identify how they can be more efficient in the use of their few resources. Over the years, this scarcity has also shaped a unique feature of Danish culture that has also positively contributed to innovative mindsets. As Martin remarked, there is

> a very big "Do-It-Yourself" culture in Denmark at all levels of society. This means that a lot of people in companies are also engaged in using their hands from time to time, which has a positive spillover effect on the ways that people approach problems and try to try to solve them.

This handy self-reliance combined with the small population, widespread egalitarianism, and lack of hierarchy found in Danish companies means that people often trust one another to a large degree. This occurs because people and governments are generally viewed as reliable and because people can get to know each other more easily. As Martin from Denmark told us, this tight-knit and collaborative atmosphere serves to foster innovation as

> you can easily go from one end to the other without the need of very big networks. People have access to different kinds of resources through these networks and are sort of connected to many different types of organizations, resources, and competencies.

There is also another historical aspect that shaped Danish culture. Traditionally, there were two types of Danish people: seafarers and farmers. The confluence of these two occupations helped to fuel the different types of innovation we see today in Denmark. The seafarers, of course, bought home the diverse ideas and products that they discovered over the course of their travels. They also inherently contributed a sense of curiosity, risk-taking, and adventurousness associated with all seafaring people. Aside from these cultural features, these people were also responsible for the origin of the shipping industry, including the world's largest integrated shipping company, Maersk. The shipping industry then became an early adopter of automation logistics, which later led to digitization. This innovation later lent itself the structuring of Danish society and gov   ernment, with digitization helping to closely link the government to corporations.

The other half of society – the farming community – was also just as important to the formation of modern Denmark. Namely, they helped to reinforce and guide the country's early land-based innovations and fostered a cultural affinity for sustainability. In the early days, the country's lack of natural resources meant that farmers had to be quite innovative to use the few resources at their disposal in the most efficient way possible. Because people were rather trusting and collaborative, these innovations did not remain secretive and siloed, but rather the community shared these ideas and build upon them. Many of Denmark's strongest industries today, including the wind turbines and water pumps, began in this fashion and due to the region's relative desolation. Martin described how this process was then scaled up to describe the whole of the Danish economy. He said:

> We have a huge number of small- and medium-sized enterprises that don't really entertain themselves with making turnkey solutions of any kind. Rather, they focus on very narrow specialization and issues in the market and become very, very good at providing, for instance, software for running batteries in vehicles, as an example. So, within these broader pump and wind turbine industries, there are a lot of companies that actually deliver very specialized knowledge, very specialized products into those value chains and are very good at that.

This precision knowledge model was then replicated in the modern era with big life science pharmaceutical companies, including Novo Nordisk.

Yet another example of a small and resource-poor, yet highly innovative, country can be found in Switzerland. Prior to World War II, Switzerland was a barren place that lacked the fertile lands of neighboring France, who were quite wealthy due to the variety of crops that they were able to produce. According to Nicolas Musy, a Swiss national and the founder of The Swiss Centers in

Shanghai and China Integrated, the early lack of opportunity in the country initially led to a mass exodus of the population. He elaborated that at one point, "Switzerland's main export was people, either as soldiers or as immigrants." Thus, the impetus was on those who stayed in the country to innovate and find unique value for themselves in the absence of abundant natural resources. This led to a certain degree of interdependence, but also a very diverse ecosystem that featured several small corporations that both cooperated and competed with one another. This naturally occurring co-opetition meant that high-quality precision industries evolved over time, with each small company innovating and refining their own products in an attempt to bring better products to the market.

One famous example of these industries featuring incremental innovation and refinement is the Swiss watchmaking industry. In another example of how historical events shaped national innovation, Nicolas points out that the original watchmaking expertise was not born in Switzerland, but rather:

> It was introduced by Protestant immigrants from France because they were not welcome in a Catholic country. They came to Switzerland and started watchmaking. But from there on, watchmaking also generated a lot of innovation in the product itself and naturally in the production methods on how to make those watches, so people developed machines.

Eventually these intricate machines were creatively repurposed for other industries such as knives, textiles, and even semiconductors (whose production originated in Switzerland), which to this day remain unmatched in terms of quality and precision.

CULTURE AND RELIGION

Another historical factor that has shaped innovative cultures is religion. For example, the seventeenth and eighteenth centuries featured an explosion of scientists and inventors in Sweden, particularly in terms of engineering. Mats Harborn, a Swedish national and the President of Scania China, shared that this dramatic uptick in regional innovation coincided with the gradual conversion from Catholicism to Lutheranism around the same time. According to Catholic tradition, the worthiest pursuit of one's life is to glorify and worship God. Departing from this ideology, Martin Luther inspired the strong work ethic associated with Protestants by declaring that people can be good Christians if they engage in pursuits that help to enrich the broader society. Even today, roughly 60.2%[6] of Swedes identify as a member of the Church of Sweden, which is a part of the Lutheran sect of Protestantism. Thus, it is possible that this mass conversion helped to fuel early innovations during the Swedish Scientific Revolution by freeing the great minds of the time to pursue endeavors that helped to advance society rather than just helping the Church. Rather than investing extra resources into building bigger and more gilded houses of worship, people were suddenly creating new inventions and re-investing any money they made into new projects. As Mats from Scania notes,

> *that's what we also saw in the early industrialization, that most of these capitalists, they were not very indulgent. They were reinvesting and they felt that they were doing something for their community or for society.*

Here again we can see the historical origins of modern Swedish culture, which is widely characterized by a mantra of *Jantelagen*,[7] which means not talking about money and avoiding bragging about flashy purchases to reinforce perceptions of equality.

Israel provides another rich example of how religious influences may have helped to shape the innovative nature of various countries. Echoing our interviewees from the UAE and Denmark, Roy Chason, the Israeli founder of the consulting company KnoHao, gave us his take of why such a resource-poor country like Israel – which currently has a population of only 9 million, faces regional instability, and possesses very few natural resources – has been branded as an innovation superstar with nicknames like the "Start-up Nation" and the "Silicon Wadi." According to Roy, much of the Israeli people's innovative spirit can be traced back to the historical experiences that have shaped the Jewish people. As one of the world's oldest religions and civilizations, this tight-knit group was without a homeland and migrated continuously around the world. "For example, my father was born in Greece, but his ancestors were in Spain. My father spoke Spanish at home. Jews spread all over the world and never attained political power. Jews essentially had to innovate to survive," recounts Roy. Historically, this innovation was linked to their transient existence: they began by engaging in commodities trading before getting into money lending. A key characteristic of the Jewish people throughout history was adapting to new environments and innovating to survive, which is still firmly embedded in the Israeli DNA.

Aside from historical experiences, Roy Chason also contended that Judaism itself shaped cultural traditions that fuel innovation. The earliest temple in ancient Israel, which served as the center of Jewish culture and spirituality, was completely destroyed twice by external forces. This lack of a central place to gather had two profound effects on Jewish (and later, Israeli) culture. As Roy shared with us:

As the Jewish people had their Temple in Jerusalem destroyed on two occasions, all that remained to take with them in their exile was the Torah – the Jewish written bible. This way they could maintain and transfer on their age-old traditions from one generation to another despite being displaced. Literacy was therefore a necessity. There was no longer any hierarchy in the religion like in the Temple period, and so the contribution of the entire community in their collective rituals was an important value. In addition to the written law (Torah) which is static, Jews have the Talmud, which is the tradition of oral law, a law which constantly evolves. Even in modern times, religious students enthusiastically discuss and argue over Talmudic passages, in small learning groups called Havrutas, *constantly challenging and questioning the meaning of each paragraph. Both Jewish study and prayer could now travel anywhere and be done in virtually any place, whether in*

the home or a small room, instead of large established
churches or mosques that are the traditional and holy
places of worship for Christianity and Islam.

This strong emphasis on education and flat hierarchy continues to be a key cornerstone of modern Israeli culture. Moreover, as mentioned, since Talmudic law constantly evolved and was being debated, we see a similar phenomenon in modern-day Israel where people feel perfectly comfortable to disagree and debate with one another if they see things differently. As a result, people constantly question and alter the status quo. Indeed, according to Dr Erin Meyer's book, *The Culture Map*, Israel ranks among the countries that most value direct negative feedback and confrontation. This early abolishment of hierarchy following the abandonment of physical temples has also resulted in Israeli culture being highly egalitarian and informal. This informality is expressed in various ways, ranging from the lack of a filter in everyday conversations, the manner of dress, and the fact that all citizens refer to top-ranking officials by their first names or even nicknames. Roy explained that this brusque demeanor has led Israelis born in the country to adopt the designation of *Sabra*, which is the fruit of the cactus. He explained:

A cactus fruit is kind of sweet inside and outside is very
thorny. The Israeli mentality is one born from Israel's rough
environment. It's all desert and there was essentially noth-
ing cultivated on the land. We had to grow everything from
zero while defending the country against our neighbors.
That created a very prickly exterior – Israelis are tough.
We say what we think. We constantly challenge author-
ity. This is, again, connects back to the historical part in
our religion, constantly challenging the status quo, and not
accepting authority.

Thus, although the Jewish culture clings to strong traditions in terms of fundamental values, Israel's historical and religious roots have led it to become a society that is more open to adaptation, change, and innovation than many others. The fruits of these unique cultural elements are apparent through the advent of disruptive technologies that contribute to a more sustainable world, including real slaughter-free meat grown in flasks and milk developed in the lab that mimics the nutritional value of cow's milk almost identically. In addition, the egalitarian and informal aspects of the culture are also transmitted into corporate culture. In Israeli startups, even the most junior staff members are encouraged and even expected to argue back with their superiors when they disagree with something. This allows innovation to flourish as it is widely accepted that the lower-ranking employees frequently have access to technological or customer-centric knowledge that can help the company to succeed. In Israel, it is never assumed that the CEO universally has the most knowledge or the best ideas.

CULTURAL ASPECTS

In our research and discussions with executives around the world, a consistent factor that emerged when explaining why certain countries and cultures were more innovative than others was an emphasis on education. As an example, Jerry from Cargill noted that the USA has some of the best universities in the world and counts among its residents the most Nobel Prize winners of any country. He opined that this is, in part, because the top universities are privately run, allowing them to attract the best professors from around the world. Martin from Denmark noted that his country's provision of free education for all has also helped to provide the brainpower to fuel innovation. David Wang, the China president of the Swiss company Buhler, was also emphatic that education played an oversized role in Switzerland's innovation journey, suggesting that "despite its small size, Switzerland has some very top universities worldwide. Education is one of the most critical factors in fostering innovation in any country." Nicolas, a Swiss native, echoed this point by noting how the local universities are close contenders with top universities in the USA and England, whereas "France, Germany, and Italy, all the big neighbors that are multiple times the economic size of Switzerland, remain in the second tier in terms of science and technology."

The instrumental impact of education on shaping innovative societies has roots that run much deeper than modern-day elite

universities. As an example, Sweden was among the first to introduce compulsory education in 1845, requiring students from all
socioeconomic backgrounds to attend at least six years of school.
This helped not only to further instill the sense of equality that
Sweden is famous for, but as Mats, a Swedish native told us, this
policy

> *made it possible to liberate the brains of everyone, no
> matter if you came from very poor backgrounds or more
> privileged backgrounds. With compulsory education ...
> teachers were encouraged to identify and encourage stu-
> dents that were very adept at studies.*

When considered in conjunction with the rise of Lutheranism
discussed earlier (and with it, open access to the Bible), education
became more accessible to a wider cross-section of society, leading
to more diverse and innovative ideas. As people were liberated to
think their own thoughts and follow their own passions, innovation followed. As Mats from Sweden described:

> *I meet a lot of very innovative people in Swedish indus-
> try and academia and one thing that runs through all of
> them is huge passion. They are so committed; it seems like
> this is their calling and their life's purpose to solve a given
> problem.*

This educated population also translated into a culture of
empowerment and responsibility for solving problems. Rather
than appealing to those with higher status or education to solve
problems, common people take it upon themselves to find a novel way to resolve issues. This resilience and self-reliance in the
face of obstacles has also lent itself to another famous Swedish
attribute – the pursuit of quality. Often, low-quality products
happen when one cannot figure out how to alter a design to fit
within the budgetary or production constraints. When the population is highly educated and unafraid to take on challenges,
longer-lasting, high-quality products are created because people
take pride in finding a way to achieve good products and good
designs within the constraints. Of course, this methodology itself
is another form of innovation.

Fast-forward to today, and many of the most innovative Swedish companies are involved not in design or high-quality products, but rather in technology. Examples include Spotify, the digital music service, and Tobii, a world leader in eye-tracking innovation that can be applied to gaming, virtual reality, heavy machinery operation, and scientific research. Mats from Sweden attributes the rise of this non-traditional sector to changes made in the Swedish educational system around the 1950s. Among them, the new curriculum fosters critical thinking and students are taught to openly question authority and the status quo. The educational system also focuses on protecting childhood and encouraging non-academic activities like sports because, as Mats notes, the government recognizes "that it is in that period when you're young and you're playful that you also develop your sort of innovative way of thinking."

The UAE is another example of a country that has prioritized education, particularly in recent years. In its pursuit to build a true knowledge-based economy, the country has invested heavily in education and has succeeded in growing the adult literacy rate from 53.5% in 1975 to 93.2% in 2015.[8] The UAE provides free education to its citizens and has made cutting-edge updates to its public-school systems on an almost yearly basis. In fact, as our Emirati interviewee, Omar, shared with us, the public-school system was among the best prepared for switching to remote learning during the COVID-19 pandemic. Omar recounted that:

> The UAE previously had exercised a drill about two years before the pandemic hit, so they were already prepared on how to engage in remote learning and had already trained over 20 instructors who were given the tools on how to start this. During the pandemic, these 20 instructors were able to teach other schools, including 55 private schools, how to adapt to digital learning.

Innovation in Israel has also been propelled by education. For one, they committed to building a series of world-class universities, including Hebrew University, Haifa, and the engineering school, Technion. Aside from educating the public, these universities also have very strong partnerships with the private sector for the purposes of creating new patents and technologies. Roy from KnoHao contends that the country's small size helps to aid close connections between organizations and academia that foster new ideas.

Aside from university education, however, Israel also departs from other innovative economies in their broad definition of where learning and education can be sourced. For one, there is a widespread agreement that the younger generations have much more knowledge and expertise in technology given the constant rate of change. Roy contended that in this fast-paced world,

> you have to give power and respect to your younger employees and let them feel like their say is as important as yours if you want to innovate. This is essentially very important for the startup culture.

Israel also boasts a second unique source of education: compulsory military service. Everyone – both men and women – must serve in the military at a young age. According to Roy, the lessons they learn through this service imprint them with unique cultural features including self-sufficiency, confidence, maturity, and comfort with risk-taking. As a result, Israeli youth largely do not fear rejection or failure. Applying these characteristics to the entrepreneurial setting, Roy notes that

> one of the basic tenants of startup companies is kind of "fake it until you make it." Even if your product is not ready for the market, you must show your customer or your investor that you are ready. The confidence that they gain from the military time is important for this.

A final lesson that can be gleaned about the importance of learning for innovation is that young or developing nations should not only focus on building world-class education systems within the country, but also should be looking outwards to learn from the successes of others. As an example, the first seaport and airport in the UAE were established in a less well-known Emirate called Sharjah. Dubai and the other Emirates saw Sharjah's success and were quick to implement and build upon it themselves. From the earliest days of the country's formation, the UAE has also consistently looked outwards learn from the development of countries like Singapore and South Korea as these places are also relatively small and lack considerable natural resources. Omar explained the parallels between the UAE and Singapore in particular, noting that:

> *Singapore and the UAE are almost the same size, have the same population number, and the same issue of no resources. The UAE wondered, how did Singapore become this knowledge-based economy? They have nothing. They've never had a single big business there, so how did they become this big success?*

To better understand this phenomenon, since the early 1990s, a delegation of people from different sectors of the UAE go to study each year and learn from the government of Singapore through the UAE-Singapore Council, a formalized program of knowledge exchange. An early innovation that resulted from this exchange was the Dubai Shopping Festival (DSF). The creator of this yearly event lived in Singapore for a long time and got the idea for an international shopping event after visiting the Hong Kong Shopping Festival. He later brought this idea home and adapted it to the Arab culture and climate, leading to a highly successful initiative that attracts scores of tourists to the UAE each year. For example, the DSF's 25th edition in 2019 was the most successful to date, involving over 4,000 retail outlets and 3,847 events that attracted over 10 million attendees over its 38-day duration.[9] Thus, looking back on the history and the deliberate efforts of the UAE to learn from Singapore's success, it is no wonder that people now make so many parallels between Dubai and the Asian city state.

Ever the visionary, Sheikh Mohammed, the ruler of Dubai and Vice President of the UAE, does not only hope to learn from other governments, but also seeks inspiration for how to run his government from private companies. Omar shares more about this innovative approach:

> *It comes from the adoption of the whole concept of 10x-ing or achieving exponential growth. Google, for example, has the X-Moonshot Factory. They ask, "how can we plan for the next 50 years? How can we solve the*

problems that are coming next?" Then they sit around and think of the craziest ideas and solutions. Sheikh Mohammed surrounds himself with a similar type of forward-thinking geniuses. He surrounds himself with a strong network of people who come from companies like Google, Apple, etcetera, and they sit around him, and they give him ideas. He does this because he wants to run the government like a corporation. There is a reason it is known as Dubai, Inc.

One of the innovations that emerged from this collaborative form of governance was the implementation of the E-Government. It was mandated that most of the government services were to be completed via websites and all the information the public needed had to be found on websites. After this process was completed, the government then moved the goalpost again to make the shift to a mobile government. Today, for example, traffic accidents are reported entirely via mobile applications. The next step for the government is to remove human interaction altogether from many processes by increasing efficiency of transactions and moving to a completely digital platform. The UAE has continued to leverage innovation to achieve several goals, including opening the Museum of the Future, a Centre for Government Innovation, a Solar Park, and the world's first 3D-printed building.[10]

Although the most innovative nations have truly committed to the importance of education, some people are concerned that modern education systems may be dampening innovation going forward. For example, Mats from Sweden worries that the more stringent grade requirements for joining engineering schools in his country today may be filtering out the late bloomers or the people who are naturally curious. In doing so, they may lose to the playful freethinkers that often produce the most disruptive innovations.

NATIONAL SECURITY AND STABILITY

Another less-frequently discussed antecedent of innovation that came up over the course of our research was the importance of living in a society that was rather stable and secure. This is perhaps most visible in the rise in innovation in Switzerland over the last several decades. Switzerland is famous for its permanent and self-imposed foreign policy of neutrality that was formally recognized by the League of Nations in 1920.[11] Since this time (and, indeed, for many years before), the small nation has refused to be involved in armed or political conflicts between other nations to preserve security and peace. As a result of this policy, Switzerland has avoided involvement in the major world conflicts and has been able to keep their economy growing despite what was going on around them. When combined with the urgency presented by the small size of the nation and small number of natural resources, its people are both protected and incentivized to innovate. As David from Buhler suggested, "That [stability] gave people peace and time to work on things and develop high-quality craftsmanship. When you think of Swiss-Made, you think of something that is precise and reliable."

Singapore is another secure haven that has been repeatedly praised for its highly attractive living conditions that attract top talent from around the world.[12] These efforts to create an innovative ecosystem have resulted in the island city state surpassing even Silicon Valley as the best place for start-up talent in the world according to the Startup Genome's Global Ecosystem Ranking Report 2017. In addition to targeted government support for cutting-edge industries like biomedical sciences, sustainability, and the digital economy (including a staggering US$13.9 billion earmarked for R&D capabilities[13]), Singapore also ensures stability and limits risk by pursuing innovation using a "sandbox approach." This entails allowing solutions, programs, or business models (e.g., big data exchange and FinTech applications) to be trialed in a limited, yet lightly regulated, fashion before approving large-scale roll-outs. All these initiatives are enabled by a strong and centralized government.

The Middle East, unfortunately, is notorious for conflicts and unrest. In its fledgling days as a new nation, the UAE recognized the importance of security and peace to create an ecosystem that fosters innovation. One policy they adopted was to ensure that the military members and police force are among not only the highest paid people in the country, but also among their colleagues doing similar jobs around the world. In addition to high salaries, military and police families have also traditionally been provided free accommodation, water, electricity, telephone services, education, and healthcare. Collectively, these benefits ensure that there is very little incentive for these citizens to be tempted by corruption or turning a blind eye to others. It comes as no surprise, then, that the UAE is tied for 21st place as one of the cleanest countries in the world according to Transparency International's *Corruption Perceptions Index 2020*.[14]

In addition to this, many of the UAE's top government leaders were educated and trained in elite schools like West Point in the USA or Sandhurst Military Academy in the UK. As Omar from the UAE shared with us, during their education

> *the leaders are instilled with those values that come from a place like West Point or Sandhurst. That's why you have a culture that is permeated with safety and security and this type of environment creates a whole culture of people committed to make this country succeed.*

This policy of ensuring stability and security was later enhanced by high levels of investment into cybersecurity. This has allowed the government to monitor and sanction people who try to destabilize the society and promote discrimination from behind the relative anonymity of the internet. Unlike other parts of the world, few are tempted to express xenophobic, anti-Semitic, or Islamophobic opinions when the penalty is 100,000 dirhams (over $27,000) and five years in jail.

In another part of the Middle East, innovation has been greatly impacted by attempts to increase national security. Namely, Israel has been under constant threat of attack from neighboring countries since the nation's founding. As the population of the country, particularly in the early years, was quite small, Israelis were forced to innovate in order to have a technological advantage over rivals. As Roy from Israel shared with us,

> *from day one, Israel's military had to gain a technological edge over its neighbors and constantly innovate. And that transcended into the private sector. A lot of the technologies which you see today in startup companies are technologies that were initially developed in the military.*

In sum, although countries vary widely in their strategies and approaches to ensure national security and stability, the common focus on creating a safe and stable environment proves to aid innovation.

LOCALIZED CLUSTERS OF INNOVATION

A final theme that emerged when studying the patterns of innovative societies around the world, and one that is corroborated by INSEAD's GII, is the importance and impact of physical clusters of innovation (usually cities) within countries. Often, this takes the form of certain cities becoming famous for a specific industry or type of innovation. Taking Switzerland as an example, the city of Lausanne focuses on entrepreneurial startups and new technologies, Zürich has traditionally been the home of academic innovation and top universities, and Geneva has focused on scientific advancements.

Traditionally, many of these localized clusters emerged organically because of historical factors. This was certainly the case in the USA over the last century. Examples of US clusters include the emergence of aerospace, internet, and coffee innovations in Seattle, internet and technology innovations in Silicon Valley, and automobile innovations in Detroit. The emergence of these hubs then became more entrenched in the latter part of the twentieth century as universities in these areas began providing specialized degrees that matched the needs of local corporations (e.g., petroleum engineering degrees in Louisiana and Texas as the oilfield was centralized there). This also extended to employee development within companies themselves. Namely, big companies will often extensively train local talent to meet their specialized needs and compensate them well even in the absence of a university degree (e.g., aerospace machinists). The presence of the large companies also attracts auxiliary industries, which further fuels specialized expertise and innovation in a specific area. This can be quite efficient, as highlighted by the problems faced by decentralized countries. For example, Hellmut Schutte, a German national and the Former Dean of INSEAD in Singapore and

CEIBS in China, explained that people coming to Germany to do business are

> *constantly in the wrong place because some companies are in Stuttgart, others in Cologne, others in Munich and Bremen and Hamburg and Berlin. Berlin has only one company, which is a larger company, and that's the German Railway, which is state owned. Everything else is somewhere around Germany. Has this been good to build innovative ecosystems? No, I don't think so.*

In contrast, there are at least two reasons that the localized innovation hubs in the USA have certain unique advantages as compared to other parts of the world. The first is that both people and companies can freely move from one physical location to another – in the case of people, even one industry to another – and bring these new ideas with them. For example, anyone can be from one part of the country, get educated in another, and start working in a third location, promoting diversity and the exchange of ideas along the way. In many places around the world (e.g., China), this is not so easy to do. In the case of companies, we are seeing many companies changing the location of their headquarters to pursue more favorable taxes and business conditions – most notably with many Californian companies relocating to Texas and Florida. A second advantage of the hubs in the USA is that in modern cities now host several different start companies hailing from different industries, leading to the cross-pollination of ideas. Our American interviewee, Cameron Johnson, offered Seattle and Silicon Valley as examples:

> *Seattle, for example, is known for Microsoft, Starbucks, Amazon, and Boeing. You get all these engineers together in the same physical hub. Even when you have an ecosystem and you have different companies: aerospace, software and selling books online, for example (which generally don't have anything to do with each other), but when you get these engineers talking, they look at different ideas, different ways of doing business. They might say "Hey, I didn't realize that concept. How are you doing this?*

*What are you doing over there?" And again, this is the
innovation that has driven the US forward in many ways.
When you look at Silicon Valley, historically, companies
are doing all kinds of things. Oracle is doing enterprise
software, Apple is doing something different, Facebook
is even something further, Google is search online, and
so on. Then people move from company to company and
start talking to each other, this is the innovation drive. The
ecosystem really pushes things forward.*

In other economies that are hoping to accelerate their development, these hubs or clusters are often artificially created. One
example of this occurred in Dubai. To incentivize multinational
companies to set up headquarters in the city, the government of
Dubai created various industry-specific Free Zones. These Free
Zones offered multinational companies several benefits including
100% foreign ownership, numerous tax exemptions, and international law. There are clusters created for universities, internet companies, media companies, and manufacturing, to name a few. Omar
from Dubai told us a fascinating story about how the country's
leaders used an innovative approach to attract foreign businesses
to the area:

*Everything was built, meaning the actual physical build-
ings were built in Dubai Media City and Dubai Internet
City. But nobody came – for 6 months they didn't have one
single tenant because at the time these areas seemed far
from the city. It seemed like it was isolated and there was
not going to be much happening. So, Sheikh Mohammed
called his good friend, Bill Gates, and offered to give him
one building rent-free for 50 years. The second thing he
offered was all the contracts from the government to
evolve e-government .... So it was a no-brainer for Bill
Gates. The incentive for Microsoft to be in the UAE was
about growing and scaling the business from the UAE to
other Arab countries around the region .... Next thing you
know, Microsoft came. And when Microsoft goes anywhere, everybody else follows. Nobody else was given that*

sort of incentive, but today there's not a single multinational on the Fortune 500 that is not already in the UAE.

In sum, localized hubs or clusters of innovation can either arise naturally or be planned to use strategic government incentives. The advantages of these clusters are the cross-pollination of innovative ideas among workers and the reinforcement of specialized knowledge and industries. It may be particularly useful in terms of innovation if people and companies are able to freely move over time to gain exposure to fresh ideas, ways of thinking, and incentives.

CONCLUSION

Different countries around the world have emerged as innovation powerhouses at various points throughout history. By examining the historical events and cultural attributes of the countries currently reigning as most innovative, we were able to uncover several intriguing patterns. For one, the physical environment and availability of natural resources (or lack thereof) have played a decisive role in driving people to be more creative in how they solve problems. Aside from the outliers of the USA and China, having a comparatively small population size also acts as a driver of innovation. Cultural characteristics including certain religious tenets, positive risk-taking attitudes, self-reliance, and egalitarianism also help to foster innovative mindsets. Countries that prioritize education and national security are also more likely to be more innovative. Finally, we noted that often innovative countries have diverse clusters of innovation, and that it is best when people can move between these clusters to cross-pollinate ideas. Population diversity is very important.

LEARNING POINTS

History and Environment

There are various ways that historical events and features of the physical environment can shape the innovativeness of a people or nation. We can distinguish between rich resources countries both natural resources and population size. Among these countries are the USA and China. However, some small countries can also reach high levels of innovation by becoming knowledge-based economies. Immigration can be a source of innovation, but it also requires a receptive culture that accept failure as the natural path to success.

Culture and Religion

Religion and history shape cultural characteristics and norms. Protestant religions promote a strong work ethic. Judaism fosters attributes that aid innovation including risk-taking, tolerance of failure, self-reliance, cooperation, egalitarianism, informality, and a lack of hierarchy.

Education and Continuous Learning

Access to free schooling and high-quality education (particularly for people from all levels of socioeconomic status) is important to fuel the critical thinking and brain power needed for innovation. Education should incorporate values like empowerment, responsibility for solving problems, critical thinking, and challenging the status quo. It is also important that young or developing nations learn from the successes of others. All the countries we studied have education as a top priority.

National Security and Stability

National security and stability are critical to foster a safe space for innovation to emerge. Companies can operate in a stable business environment and plan long-term investments. Security and stability can be facilitated in many ways, including internal security, external defense, or neutrality. An interesting case is Israel, which suffers from external threats but has created a safe haven inside the country.

Localized Clusters of Innovation

Localized clusters of innovation help led to precision innovation and deep knowledge, and the movement of people and companies within and between locations helps to fuel innovation through idea exchange. Some clusters emerge organically like Seattle, Silicon Valley, Detroit, Boston, and Texas in the USA. Other clusters are the result of planned government actions like Shanghai, Shenzhen, and Tianjin in China. Singapore and UAE are examples where the whole country serves as a cluster.

NOTES

1. Meyer, E. (2015). *The culture map: Decoding how people think, lead, and get things done across cultures.* New York, NY: Public Affairs.

2. https://www.cargill.com/about/research/research-development

3. https://www.ceibs.edu/video-podcast/19797

4. https://www.sifma.org/about/our-markets/

5. https://www.dst.dk/en/Statistik/emner/befolkning-og-valg/befolkning-og-befolkningsfremskrivning/folketal

6. https://culturalatlas.sbs.com.au/swedish-culture/swedish-culture-religion

7. https://www.bbc.com/worklife/article/20191008-jantelagen-why-swedes-wont-talk-about-wealth

8. https://knoema.com/atlas/United-Arab-Emirates/topics/Education/Literacy/Adult-literacy-rate

9. https://dubaitourism.getbynder.com/m/3e56c8625ed93ce0/original/DTCM-ANNUAL-REPORT-2019-EN.pdf

10. https://u.ae/en/about-the-uae/the-uae-government/government-of-future/innovation-in-the-uae

11. https://time.com/3695334/switzerland-neutrality-history/

12. https://www.cnbc.com/2017/08/30/singapore-is-pushing-hard-to-be-a-center-for-innovation.html

13. https://www.forbes.com/custom/2018/08/13/singapore-a-global-hub-for-innovation/

14. https://www.transparency.org/en/cpi/2020/index/nzl

3

INNOVATION IN CHINA

*[Chinese people] take existing products and services,
whether they already exist in China or from other countries, and they adapt them to the local market. They make
them better. They make them faster, bigger.*

— *Roy Chason, KnoHao*

INTRODUCTION

A review of INSEAD's Global Innovation Index over the years reveals that China has made a notable upward rise, moving from 17th in 2018 to 14th in 2019. Similarly, the World Economic Forum's 2019 Global Competitiveness Report ranked the nation as 28th in the world, earning particularly high scores in macroeconomic stability, market size, and health of its human capital. China has also been more efficient with its innovation investments, pulling ahead as a leader in patents, industrial designs, trademarks, and high-tech exports.[1] Importantly, it has also been recognized as an education leader.

In this chapter, we do a deep-dive analysis on Chinese innovation. As with the previous chapter, we will explore historical and cultural factors that have influenced innovation in China. We will also describe how the methodology of innovation differs as compared to other parts of the world before highlighting several modern examples of disruptive innovation in China. Finally, we will conclude by summarizing the barriers facing Chinese innovation before offering some lessons learned from elsewhere in the world that might help to overcome these obstacles.

HISTORY OF INNOVATION IN CHINA

Any serious discussion of China often begins with praise and respect for its long and rich history of innovation. Over its thousands of years as a civilization, China has developed numerous inventions that have fundamentally altered human life, including paper making, gunpowder, printing, and the compass.[2] Mats Harborn, a Swedish national and the President of Scania China, sees many parallels between the historical innovations of China and Europe given that both traditionally focused on high-quality products. As an example, he cited

> the way that China and later Japan refined the method of joining wood without nails or screws is a fantastic innovation coming from the pursuit of quality and long-lasting things.

Roy Chason, an Israeli native and founder of the learning company, KnoHao, also sees historical similarities between China and the Jewish people. For example, both societies are extremely entrepreneurial and adaptive to change. Moreover, he notes that "there are many Chinese living outside of mainland China, in Southeast Asia, and all around the world. That's very similar to the Jewish history." As a result of this early global exposure, China brought home new ideas while retaining a consistent cultural core stemming from its long history and deeply rooted traditions that fuel innovation.

Over time, China settled into agriculture before embarking on another wave of ambitious change in the late 1970s, this time focusing on transforming the economy into a manufacturing powerhouse. This initiative has been extremely successful, with more than 800 million people being lifted out of poverty, GDP growth in the double-digits, and significant year-on-year improvement in health and education outcomes since the early 1980s.[3] As noted by Kenneth Yu, the former President of 3M China, the government has done a commendable job in the last two decades of the twentieth century to focus on productivity and commercialization to feed the world's largest population. He believes that "they did the right thing at the time by promoting industrialization, manufacturing, and creating an atmosphere for foreign countries and companies to come in and invest." As with the UAE, some of these reforms were inspired when one of the country's early leaders, Deng Xiaoping, visited Singapore in 1978 and was impressed with the rapid progress he witnessed.[4] Namely, he viewed the combination of support for private businesses and social stability as key drivers of economic development. Deng Xiaoping later applied this model to China.

In the early years of China's opening up and reform, many centralized production units in the government were converted into large state-owned enterprises (SOEs) that have also gone through various stages of development over time.[5] As the primary role of these organizations is to ensure public access to goods and services and to promote the objectives of the central government,[6] these giant corporations have faced little pressure to innovate. One Chinese executive at an environmental agency we spoke to elaborated on this idea further, stating that

> *state-owned enterprises don't worry about going bank-*
> *rupt given that they dominate the market as monopolies*
> *and hence don't have to rack their brains to innovate. In*
> *contrast, private companies face a big crisis so that they*
> *spare no efforts to find a way out.*

Private-sector market leaders face intense competition and the fear that they could be replaced at any time by newcomers, forcing them to use their vast resources to innovate and capture new markets. As a result, Chinese private companies traditionally tend to be more innovative than SOEs. Owing to decades of comparative safety, many Chinese SOEs now have entrenched corporate cultures that prioritize compliance, rigid chains of command, and limited risk taking.

However, in recent years the government has made concerted efforts to make these SOEs more agile and responsive to changing market conditions. For example, one executive noted that "the state has realized this problem and is promoting mixed ownership reform, requiring some state-owned enterprises and central enterprises to distribute some shares to private enterprises." The goal, then, is that this dual accountability will increase pressure to innovate and alter the company cultures in a way that fosters creativity. These organizations face formidable challenges to becoming truly innovative, including strong hierarchical leadership, an unwillingness to tolerate failure, and barriers to open and cross-functional communication. Jonathan Woetzel, a Senior Partner and the Director of the Global Institute at McKinsey, suggested that a first step to helping SOEs in this transformation is to give the employees working in these firms more autonomy and the ability to alter their daily circumstances. The primary obstacle to doing this, he believes, is the fact that these organizations are not only tasked with being commercially successful, but that they must also serve non-commercial purposes related to government interests. This tends to curtail the amount of empowerment and freedom that can be given to individual employees. Jonathan explained that the reason the state invests in these sectors is because:

They are afraid if they don't own it, they might lose it,
whether it is technology, resources, or some unique claim
on society. With that comes with a whole set of responsi-
bilities which are then held in the public trust. Notably,
things like your compensation are done on behalf of the
public, which, generally speaking, makes it more difficult
to have big ranges of compensation and greater levels of
inequality, but also greater levels of risk taking. There are
some constraints when acting on behalf of the public.

Still, he pointed out, there have been instances where SOEs were
able to make highly innovative contributions. As examples, he lists
that vast high-speed rail system in China and NASA in the USA. He
noted that in these rare instances,

everybody literally in the country agreed, we are going to
allow this thing to be very innovative. We are going to
allow it to break the rules, to bring in people which they
would not have brought in otherwise, to have access to
capital which they might not otherwise get and will allow
them to innovate. That happens occasionally, but in most
state enterprises, not so much.

For the vast majority, he believes that we are getting to the point
in many different sectors that governments are increasingly allowing private companies to take over things that they originally han-
dled, including mail delivery and space travel. Kamal from NIIT
added that the rigidity of SOEs is largely derived from the late-
stage life cycles of these organizations, noting that:

Some very small startup companies are very innovative,
very agile, have good innovations and business models,
and they use digital technologies to add value to customer
and new value propositions. They create a minimum
viable product that they keep testing, experimenting, and
learning and iterating and reiterating over time until it
becomes a perfect product. At the same time, you see a
lot of companies which are not innovative. They're stuck

in their old way of doing things, being in that same space,
not looking at how to use digital technologies, how do
they adapt to change. They remain stuck. In the long run
the organizations which are agile, which can adapt faster
to the change, are innovative, are going to be the front
runners.

In addition to these changes, in the recent decades China has
realized that continued prosperity will mean that the nation is on
a path to follow other countries like South Korea who originally
rose to prominence through the provision of cheap manufacturing
labor. Today, the onus is on China to continue to innovate and
change, and it has already made remarkable strides in this regard
by moving from being the factory of the world to an era of leap-
frogged technologies and global expansion. Cameron Johnson, an
American and Partner at the China-based consulting company, Tidalwave Solutions, highlighted several areas where China is already
far ahead of Western countries, including business model innovation, electric vehicles (EVs), and FinTech. Given that China does
not have well-established systems for credit cards and manufacturing technology for gas-powered vehicle production, they were
able to skip these altogether and move directly into more future-
oriented technologies without having to first dismantle entrenched
systems, vested interests, and old ways of thinking. All of this works
to China's advantage as they move forward, particularly in these
sectors. In the next section, we will consider the current landscape
in China, highlighting how the process of innovation in the country
is rather unique before giving an overview of notable examples of
modern Chinese innovation.

INNOVATION IN TODAY'S CHINA

The modern Chinese business environment is perhaps best
described as one of fierce competition and breakneck speed. It is
also much more dynamic than its Western counterparts. Owing to
its rapid progress and unique environment, there are several lessons that the world at large can take from modern China. To this
end, in this section we will delve into the mindsets and business

methods that drive innovation in the country before highlighting noteworthy corporate examples of Chinese innovation and creativity. We will illustrate that innovation takes place across the full gamut of the Chinese economy, including technology, services, and manufacturing. As Roy from Israel summarizes, "in private sector companies, we see a clear trend towards innovation. We see it across all industries in China."

Jerry from Cargill argues that there has never been a better time for China to take on the pursuit of innovation. As evidence of this, he pointed to record-breaking historical numbers in terms of R&D investment, academic papers published, patents, and number of schools that Chinese people have graduated from around the world. The Chinese government has also taken many recent steps to protect the intellectual property of local companies. David Wang, the President of Buhler China, also identified various reasons for China's recent strides toward innovation, chief among them being its giant population that is highly educated, including a large number of engineers. He contrasts this with other large world populations, such as India, where innovation is hampered by restrictive religious beliefs, and a stringent government bureaucracy that blocks the flow of ideas.

Jari Grosse-Ruyken, the Co-Founder and Managing Partner of Shanghai-based hivetime Consulting, made an astute observation connecting China's current ethos of innovation and Deng Xiaoping's famous trial-and-error approach of economic reform.[7] Just as local experiments in the past were not only tolerated, but replicated in other areas if successful, small businesses in China today are collectively engaging in small scale experiments with the dream of making it big. Roy from Israel calls this *incremental innovation*:

The [Chinese] take existing products and services, whether they already exist in China or from other countries, and they adapt them to the local market. They make them better. They make them faster, bigger.

Jari explains further how he sees this unique innovation process unfold in real time in Shanghai:

In my neighborhood, I see new shops opening every one or two months and many closing one or two months later.

> *From the German point of view, I would say, "hey, why didn't you do your business plan? You should have anticipated that if you don't have clients in the first two months, you will run out of cash and you will have to close." But just imagine that this is happening all over China on a large scale every day. Businesses open, they try new things, and most fail. Some go out of business, others succeed. And those that succeed are not following Western linear, long-term planning orientation, but they are very close to the pulse of the market. They are not afraid to try something crazy.*

Combining these insights, we can conclude that incremental improvements of proven concepts, immediate market feedback, and trial-and-error on a large-scale lead to innovations that emerge from the collective in China.

Martin, a Danish national and an Advisor of the Academy of Technical Sciences (ATV), acknowledged that although several Chinese companies are true innovation leaders on the worldwide stage (particularly in the field of digitalization and technology), he also suggested that China has a huge number of so-called *fast-follower companies* whose entire purpose is to mimic successful enterprises with the goal of making as much money as they can for as long as possible. This intense level of competition leads to a number of byproducts that have impacted the way business – and innovation – is done in modern China. For one, Chinese companies are much more agile and able to bring products to market at a much quicker speed than many of their multinational counterparts. In recognizing that fast followers will soon copy your successful products and undercut your market share, Chinese companies have a heightened urgency to push out new products quickly before they leak out to competitors. Such high levels of speed and agility are tolerated because many companies have been working in a high-growth and high-resource environment for many years, leading to the widespread assumption that even if the current product or initiative doesn't work, the next one will. As Martin from Denmark explained,

when you are in a situation where there's resource abun-
dance on many levels, then it becomes easier to just again
and again put something out, not having really taken the
time to consider whether or not it's something that will be
successful.

This mentality can also be traced to an idiom also attributed to Deng Xiaoping – "crossing the river by feeling stones." Rather than testing new ideas by engaging in cross-functional debates, strategy meetings, and focus groups, they are tested directly by consumers themselves. If people buy it, they make more, and if they don't, they release something new.

Many multinational organizations in China are currently experiencing intense pressure to innovate because they are now suddenly finding themselves in a mid-market challenge. Historically, these companies have sold their foreign products easily and at a premium because of their perceived quality. Today, he noted, the situation is changing:

The Chinese consumer is getting more and more picky,
more and more sophisticated, and is ever better informed.
The Chinese competition has also been quickly moving
up from the bottom of the market into the middle, and
that's where the music is. This is where they will gain the
momentum that will allow them to attack the top seg-
ment.

In response to this changing landscape, multinational CEOs are realizing that their 20-year strategy of allocating products and managing growth is no longer sustainable. Instead, these companies need to find a way to innovate and make themselves more competitive.

In the face of fierce competition and environmental complexities, CEOs must be willing to continuously adapt their management methods, organizational structures, and technology to cope with the changing tides. Other experts we spoke to emphasize the importance of the global headquarters giving decision-making autonomy to local teams through empowerment. To truly meet the needs of local customers and adapt to the changing conditions of the market, there cannot be a tight control of cash flows or a priority on extreme cost savings imposed by top management. Changjun Sun, a Consultant at TÜV Rheinland, suggested that such freedom is key, opining that

> *if Germany still controls China's operation, it will be difficult to meet the demands of the market. That is why some wise Germany-based heads in charge of some business lines have delegated much of the power to the China teams.*

To convince the headquarters that ample decision-making power is necessary at the local level, some have pointed out the fact that China makes up an overwhelming share of the business. Others have found that bluntly telling the headquarters that they cannot meet the assigned targets until they are fully empowered is a powerful message. In sum, when the CEO is designing the power structures and decision-making hierarchies in the organization, it is important for innovation that there is a high degree of delegation and empowerment among the local teams (as well as a high degree of accountability).

Similarly, Jun Wang, the country president of Oerlikon China, described how his headquarters chose to proactively respond to the simultaneous events of the COVID-19 pandemic and the rapid growth of the Chinese economy. Namely, top management realized that not only would China soon become a leader in production and the future of the industry, but that the country's strict border closures made it quite difficult to bring European executives into China. Considering these two factors, the board recognized that it would be best to have a Chinese team take charge of the operations and quickly approved a new organizational structure. Jun shares the details of the new reporting lines:

> *We will be separating P&L of the surface solution division from that of the global group, placing the 12 subdivisions of this division under direct management in China. The surface solution division was divided into 12 categories*

including automobiles and aviation, and every category is under vertical management globally. We will be applying methodologies and structures in a Chinese way, managing the surface solution divisions with a unique and efficient approach. This is an example of creatively implementing a structural alteration by turning 12 vertical subdivisions into horizontal channels.

David Ferreira, GM in China of Discovery, a financial services group listed in South Africa (and also Deputy CEO of Ping An Health Insurance Company, in which Discovery is a shareholder), agreed that this unique combination of speed, iterative improvements, and reducing the time between idea conceptualization and product launch are things that businesses around the world can learn from China. He described the shift in mindset that this requires – from delivering a complete and tested product to launching a prototype or pilot on the first try – using the example of a mobile application launch at the Chinese insurance firm at which he works. Although typically the process of developing an app in Western societies can involve over a year of design, engineering, beta-testing, and focus groups before the fully functional product is launched to the public, in China an app or "mini-program" (applet) can be designed, created, and launched in a matter of weeks. He explained:

We decided in February that we were going to do that and then we launch it in March. It probably had 10 percent of the functionality of the fully-fledged item, so it was very skinny. We identified the key things that our customers wanted, and gave them that. The customers found value in that, even though it didn't meet all their needs. We will be launching a second version in mid-May with perhaps 30 percent of the functionality of the fully-fledged item. By the end of the year, we will have realized our full vision for the app, but meanwhile we will have been serving customers for 11 months and we will have learned from them along the way.

Part of the reason this works is because the Chinese market is largely accustomed to organizations iteratively tweaking their products and services based on feedback and market testing. Thus, there is above-average patience for single-use applications and flaws. Particularly when it comes to digital products, this methodology works because the final version will either become more and more tailored to consumer needs and preferences or else will be replaced by something that does. The key takeaway for multinationals is that Chinese consumers often prefer speed to market and continuous improvement to waiting longer for a fully baked and tested product.

This form of consumer tolerance also provides its own pressures, however. As an example, many of our interviewees suggested that Chinese consumers are much more demanding and impatient as compared to other markets around the world. Jerry from Cargill explained that consumer tastes in China shift over a matter of three to four months, leading to a constant need for new product innovation. Another shift that has occurred in recent years is that Chinese consumers are becoming more sophisticated and unique in their tastes. Jerry shared that although in the past multinational products were first launched in Japan and South Korea before being released in China, today there is a more bi-directional influence between these markets. For example, because so many young people in these countries are quite busy, there have been numerous innovations in the food and beverage industry that cater to this new on-the-go lifestyle such as self-heating meals. He predicts that as the economy continues to grow, China will become more influential than its neighbors on product trends in the future. This indicates that firms doing business in China would be prudent to carefully study and respond to local preferences rather than relying on proven trends in the region.

Though speed to market is a fundamental basis of China's innovation, some interviewees questioned whether this is a sustainable approach for the long-term given the high-level of waste that such a system produces. Martin from Denmark provided a timely illustration of this waste of resources:

A consumer-based example for me is the shared bikes that were so prominent in China from 2017 onwards that really spelled out how this competition is taking place and how it creates a waste of resources, both in terms of money invested, but also in terms of material and people and time invested in trying to do this. And by this, I mean flooding the market with way more bikes than it could consume, and now you have all these bike cemeteries all around the country.

Although he and others we spoke to recognize the necessity of this approach for the country's current development stage, it is hoped that eventually this trend will transform into the production of more sustainable versions of these innovations that can be exported to the rest of the world. As examples, sustainable and affordable high-speed rails and shared biking systems would be very helpful to replicate in smaller scale economies in Europe and elsewhere in the world. Kenneth Yu from 3M believes that this should be possible one day, reminding us that

China built more railway than the rest of the world combined in, I think, less than 20 years. China learned from Germany, from France, and from Japan how to build High-Speed Rail Networks. Today, they are the teacher.

DISRUPTIVELY INNOVATIVE CHINESE COMPANIES

One recurring example of an area of disruptive Chinese innovation that came up in our interviews was the resounding success of the EV industry. Although Tesla is perhaps the biggest name in this area and has also made a large footprint in China, many of the other industry leaders are Chinese in origin, including Build Your Dreams (BYD), XPeng, and NIO. As Jari Grosse-Ruyken, the German Managing Partner of hivetime, noted:

NIO is doing an amazing job. It has not been a commercial success yet. But in terms of building a community of

followers, NIO is doing such an incredible job instilling customer centricity in every department of the company. It's quite inspiring.

Thanks to the feedback derived from consumers, each NIO car is filled with cutting-edge technology, including being able to verbally ask the car to open the windows, start the air conditioning, or connect your phone to the Bluetooth speakers.

Kenneth from 3M reminded us of that China's iterative method of innovation is also present in the EV sector. For example, BYD got its start not as a car company, but as a battery manufacturer for cell phones. To account for BYD's rapid growth and success, he contended that:

When it comes to innovation, I think they do better than we do in 3M. They are the world's biggest manufacturer of electric buses. They have no competition even in the US. Last year [during the COVID-19 pandemic], BYD became the world's biggest manufacturer for face masks. The whole country was short on masks, so they used their own resources and built 32 lines in few months, and they are all fully automatic.

In contrast to this astounding agility and market responsiveness, legacy motor companies competing in this space have very much stuck to a traditional playbook of engineering-driven innovations that focus on the internal development of high-quality products. Because of this, Jari predicts that in the coming years companies like Volkswagen in China "will feel the growing pressure from two sides, pressure from the top, and pressure from the bottom of the market."

Another area that China has made remarkable and disruptive strides in terms of innovation is in the technology sector. One key example is the ByteDance corporation, which was founded in 2012. It began with an application that used artificial intelligence to combine news articles from different internet sources and feed them to the consumer without having to hire reporters or journalists. Perhaps their most famous product, however, is the globally popular social media app, TikTok. TikTok was able to quickly overtake all the dominant Western social media platforms for a number of reasons, but chiefly because it was straightforward and easy to use. Cameron from Tidalwave also attributes ByteDance's success to its willingness to adopt new ideas and integrate strategies from around the world, even if they are unconventional for China. As examples of how it reinforces its persistent entrepreneurship culture, ByteDance rejects high levels of hierarchy within its ranks, going as far as to eschew company titles and identification numbers that reflect an employee's tenure. They realize that many of their top ideas will come from the youngest employees, and they ensure that the communication lines are open so that these ideas can be implemented in a timely manner. To maintain a transparent and efficient information exchange, they require employees to circulate the points they want to share with others in writing before meetings on the company's own enterprise messaging software, Lark (which is also sold for use in other organizations). Using this platform, employees are encouraged to directly contact anyone in the company without asking their leaders for approval. To seed new ideas, the founder also requires that all employees to actively use their applications. For example, all employees – even the senior ones – are required to post TikTok videos of themselves, thereby exposing areas of weakness and fueling ideas for new features. There is also a higher level of engagement and devotion to the product if the employees are active users of the products as well.

COMPANY SNAPSHOT

Tencent

Tencent has been a consistent leader in the Chinese internet industry since it was established in 1999. Its first innovative product was a wildly popular instant communication software product, QQ. Owing to its friendly and easy to use interface, this software managed to overtake MSN messenger as the dominant messaging application in China. In time, its other products also repeated this pattern, with QQ Games defeating competitor OurGame and Tencent Online Games defeating Shanda.

Tencent succeeded based on product innovation. In the era of mobile internet, Tencent was the fastest internet giant to transform through the introduction of WeChat. Within one year after it was first released in January of 2011, WeChat had released 11 different updates on roughly a monthly basis. These updates featured iterative improvements where users were consistently exposed to new features including Message in a Bottle, Shake, Photo Album, Circle of Friends, and the WeChat Payment System.

As a product-driven company, Tencent has implemented constant innovative management, and formed a unique product innovation system. It encourages constant innovation by organizing the firm around products rather than function. This, combined with the normative tradition of improvement via fast iterations, helps the company to react quickly and stay ahead of the competition. Part of their innovative process is also an in-depth understanding of their users. In the company, employees are encouraged to adopt a psychological approach to get to know their users even better than themselves. These consumer insights are then quickly integrated into all functions including R&D, operations, and customer service. Tencent also tolerates employee failure and encourages idea exchange and communication among employees. One example of this is the progress wall in the central work area that is updated in real time so that employees always have the latest data on hand to make decisions and product improvements.

Sources: https://www.tencent.com/en-us/; http://www.360doc.com/content/14/0815/09/15477063_402068064.shtml; https://baijiahao.baidu.com/s?id=1628679740020424527&wfr=spider&for=pc; https://baike.baidu.com/item/%E8%85%BE%E8%AE%AF%E4%B9%8B%E9%81%93/19836844?fr=aladdin

Tencent is another technology company that, while more seasoned, has innovated in ways that have fundamentally altered the daily life of Chinese citizens. Their mobile application, WeChat, was launched in 2011 as messaging app that allowed for easy group discussions. As they gained huge numbers of users – the application boasted 1.25 billion monthly active users in 2021[8] – they have continuously added new features that help to further entrench the usage of the application in all aspects of Chinese consumer lives. Together with Alibaba's Alipay application, WeChat has largely eliminated the need to carry around cash, credit cards, or even identification on a daily basis. As Cameron described,

> right now, you can buy food, you can get airplane tickets [all on a single mobile phone application]. That does not exist in the West at all. So, these are incredible innovations that the Chinese figured out that in the new world, today's world, the world of the future, you have to have those ecosystems in one place.

In addition to sending and receiving money, paying bills, renting shared bikes, and buying goods online, following the pandemic, these applications gained even more functionality as you can show your vaccination status and check to see if you have traveled through high-risk areas. Facebook is trying to create a similar integrated system, but time will tell if they are able to accomplish this.

As a result of groundwork laid by these applications and their parent companies, our interviewees agreed that the Chinese FinTech industry is at least a decade ahead of the West, where people still must carry cash, debit cards, or checks to make transactions. Because China lacked much of the old infrastructure (e.g., credit card systems, old technology and processes), they were able to skip past this and did not have to dismantle the legacy systems and mindsets before introducing the new technology. As Cameron noted, "it's not just QR codes, but it's also the fact that the government has allowed people in FinTech to take risks and to do different things." Although there has been a significant increase in government oversight into the technology industries since that interview[9] was conducted, we believe that China will continue to capitalize on its head start in the years to come. Recent reports show that it is well on its way, with the 2019 Global FinTech Adoption Index[10] by Ernst & Young naming China as the leading country in the world with digital adoption rates nearing 87% of the population.

COMPANY SNAPSHOT

JD.com

Founded in 1998, JD was the first Chinese large-scaled integrated e-commerce platform listed on the US Stock exchanged. Today, it is a member of the NASDAQ100, is a Fortune Global 500 company, and consistently ranks among the top ten internet companies in the world. JD has experienced multiple transformations over its history, changing from a focus on multi-media to e-commerce and the current JD Group. Currently, JD is not only an e-commerce platform, but also has another two major businesses: JD Finance and JD Logistics.

Aside from adhering to innovation as one of its core values, JD also emphasizes learning, constant improvement, and tolerance of failure as well as combining new concepts and technologies in its products and services. For instance, the "JD Pick-up Cabinet" was an innovative product that disrupted the last mile distribution of purchased goods. JD Finance also innovatively combines finance with technology.

Since JD entered the e-commerce market in 2004, it adopted strategies that differ from most existing platforms. As example, they choose to focus on gaining profits by lowering their internal costs and improving operating efficiency rather that single-mindedly focusing on gross margins. This has allowed them to gain market share by offering quality goods at low prices without bargaining. By expanding their user base and sales volumes, they were then able to attract more brand suppliers, leading to a virtuous cycle.

JD Logistics has also implemented several novel innovations, including improving supply chain efficiency by developing an information-based supply chain system. Using big data and cloud computing capacities, they were able to achieve an automatic distribution schedule, improving service quality significantly. JD Finance has also helped feed into the innovation of the central e-commerce platform by creating its own payment system. In addition to not being dependent on other payment systems like Alipay and gaining quicker access to funds, it has also allowed for financial integration through the advance payment of consumers, making its system more competitive.

Sources: https://www.jd.com/; https://max.book118.com/html/2018/0716/8012000074001115.shtm; https://wenku.baidu.com/view/b69898fca26925c52cc5bfac.html; https://max.book118.com/html/2018/0716/8012000074001115.shtm

There have also been several standout examples of business model innovation in other industries that have led to a complete overhaul in how business is done in these sectors. One example is Luckin coffee. Although Starbucks had already expanded broadly throughout China, Luckin was able to sweep in and very quickly open new stores (up to a peak of 4,500 in 2019) and take market share from the expensive coffee giant. Using app-based technology, Luckin lured customers with its inexpensive prices, loyalty discounts, and delivery or pick-up options. Because of a focus on takeaway or delivery through the app, they often had as little as a single employee filling orders. Although business has since shrunk considerably following their accounting scandal,[11] Starbucks and other local coffee chains were forced to innovate and create their own applications, mobile customer interfaces, and delivery schemes. As Cameron told us, this innovation did not stop at China's borders:

> *Starbucks took that learning and implemented it into the US, so if you look at the US Starbucks app, it is designed very similarly to the Chinese app. It doesn't have a delivery option per say, unless you're in New York City or another large city with that capability. But you if you're*

*at home and you want to order a Starbucks coffee, you
can just go on your app, order your coffee, and let them
know you will be there in a half hour to pick it up. That
did not exist even five years ago. That is an example of a
true innovation that started in China and was copied in
the West.*

As a final example, we note that the world's top consumer
drone manufacturer, DJI, was created in China. Although commonly associated with entertainment and photography, this company and its products have also made an innovative mark on
various sectors including logistics (e.g., Amazon deliveries) and
agriculture. On the agricultural front, these drones can use AI to
analyze environmental and weather factors and calculate the precise quantities of pesticide needed for each crop before deploying
the exact amount.

To conclude, we expect that the world is only just beginning
to see the tip of the iceberg in terms of Chinese innovation.
As Jonathan Woetzel, an American and Senior Partner at
McKinsey & Company observed,

*for any economy that is the size that China relative to the
world and has the growth potential that China does, they
almost by definition will have to be an innovation leader.
Maybe not always* the *innovation leader, but certainly* an
innovation leader in pretty much every industry.

Given its unique context, culture, and methodologies, the innovations that China will introduce stand to be markedly different
from innovations coming from other regions in the world. Namely,
Jonathan believes that these innovations will be cheaper (due to
reduced cost in human capital and supply chains), faster (because
of the impatience of consumers and accelerated pace of digital
technology), and more global (as it has traditionally been more
open to foreign investment in technology). Kenneth agrees with
this assessment, concluding that "there is no barrier to innovation
in China right now. The atmosphere is such that people are very
adaptive. This is China."

Still, others we spoke to were more tempered in their assessment, highlighting several obstacles that may be impeding Chinese innovation. In the next section, we consider some of these factors and then provide ideas on how these might be mitigated.

COMPANY SNAPSHOT

Xiaomi

The Global Mobile Internet Conference in 2010 named Xiaomi as a premier innovation-driven internet company, and over the last decade, it has become a listed company with a market value of over 200 billion RMB. It was also selected as one of the 2021 Global Top 100 Innovative Institutions released by Clarivate. In the 2020 International Appearance Design System released by World Intellectual Property Organization, Xiaomi ranked within the top five globally, becoming the first Chinese enterprise to do so. In a speech marking Xiaomi's 10th Anniversary, Lei Jun, the founder of Xiaomi, outlined "three iron rules" for Xiaomi: implementing technology-based products, retaining a low-cost, performance-centered strategy, and making the coolest products.

Xiaomi faced fierce competition when entering the smart phones industry in the early years and its most important strategy to survive was to make constant innovation. During an internal conference, Lei Jun emphasized the importance of further strengthening the company's capacity to consistently release new products and harness new technologies. Owing to such persistence, Xiaomi has shifted from MIUI to mobile phones, from single products to the layout of ecological chains, has expanded from the China domestic market to the global market, and transformed from pure e-business to the new online and offline combined retail over the last decade.

Sources: https://www.mi.com/updateBrowser/index.html; https://www.sohu.com/a/412582014_115865; https://tech.ifeng.com/c/7yvUfpAHtMc

CHALLENGES FACING INNOVATION IN CHINA

As with much of the world, Chinese industries now find themselves under increasing pressure to innovate in order to mitigate future challenges and adapt to new technologies. Underscoring the urgency of this external pressure, Xiaolin Yuan, President and CEO of Volvo Cars Asia Pacific, shared that "the world is just different now. The world has changed so much and so fast, you need to open up your mind and see different ways of doing things." One of these areas is to increase the sustainability of business models. David from Buhler said that his organization is looking to turn this into a competitive opportunity by continuously asking themselves,

> *how could we reinvent our technology to be more geared towards sustainability so that we'd be able to reduce energy consumption, water usage, reduce wastage? It is a global megatrend in our industry, and we are facing it together with our customer.*

On a larger scale, the Chinese government has issued huge incentives to help foster the manufacture and adoption of EVs[12] and is transforming the nation into a low carbon economy.[13]

Another major megatrend that many Chinese companies are grappling with is digitalization. Consumers are increasingly demanding more personalized and targeted offerings that require the use of cloud services, big data, and AI. As one example of how companies are innovating to comply with these changes, David from Buhler noted that his company has established strong automation capabilities related to software development, which have allowed them to develop a very sophisticated MES (manufacturing execution system) that works with their equipment, helping customers by "improving factory OEE through the data collection, we understand how the machine can operate more efficiently with better results."

Another issue facing both multinational and local companies in China is the slowing economy after many years of unprecedented and explosive growth. Although opportunities remain, competition is becoming fiercer and firms are needing to adapt their strategies with these altered expectations in mind. Xiaolin elaborates on the impact of these shifts in the context of his experience at Volvo Cars:

> *We've managed to sustain double digit growth year over year between 2010 and towards the end of 2021 .... Now, that may sound like a lot. But if we look at the growth of all premium brands, that's the average pace. Now, let's say the consensus arises that the growth of the market is capped at 3%, if we continue to pursue the expectation of 20% (since we've established that norm), it just isn't realistic anymore. The market has physical constraints. If you want to pursue that line of thought, your strategy requires a drastic pivot or the introduction of drastically new assets into your strategy and organization.*

To effectively adapt to these changing norms, innovation leaders cautioned against blindly latching onto new trends and fads without strategically considering whether these align with the firm's core values and competencies. One Chinese executive we spoke with warned that an unbridled R&D department can lead to over-innovation that the market may not be ready for. One key consideration is how long these trends are likely to stay around. In the automobile industry, Xiaolin suggests that remembering the core purpose of mobility is vital. Beyond this, new innovations can be adopted, but these should not be pursued haphazardly. He elaborates:

> *Fundamentally, people have not changed that much over the last 100 years .... In the beginning, there was nothing electronic in cars; it was only wood, steel, glass, and rubber. Along the way, as the material, electronic, technology, and entertainment industries developed, the automotive industry began to adopt these advancements .... Many of these technologies, however, came and left quickly. One example is DVDs and Blu Ray. Then some other technologies like streaming services and online cloud gaming came along and made those technologies obsolete. It's not just about following every trend which develops. It's about adopting what makes sense once it has a horizon.*

This example illustrates a hybrid strategy described by many of our respondents from multinational companies on reconcile the relentless pace of change and strong competition in the Chinese market with their fundamental strategy in other parts of the world. For many established brands, the key is not to be reactive and adopt every new feature that emerges on the market, but rather to be more sustainable in choosing what new directions to pursue. Although other brands may make more headlines in the short-term, companies like Volvo choose to compete in this highly dynamic and competitive atmosphere by keeping a sustainable focus on their core capabilities and improving upon these advantages by adopting selected new technologies, cooperating with the right partners, and re-defining the value chain as needed. By resisting the pressure to follow every new trend and taking the time to understand *why* something is working, Kern Peng, a Lab Head at Intel believes that companies can retain their hold as a trail blazer rather than a follower. "To be an innovation leader," Kern contended, "you have to invest the time to do it and find your own path." In this way, many of our interviewees believe that although fast change and adaptation is needed in the Chinese market, this should not be done at the expense of providing real value and remaining true to existing pillars of quality and integrity. In Xiaolin's words, "there are many roads to Rome. But we cannot take every path. We cannot actually take more than one. We have to choose one."

Another challenge facing many Chinese entrepreneurs is a difficulty in gaining access to capital. In doing so, many entrepreneurs spend lots of time and effort to educate both investors and the public, particularly in relation to novel products and services. As an example, Congwei Huang, the founder of Z-trip shared that his biggest struggle was finding investors for his internet application, which did the job previously occupied by brick-and-mortar corporations. He lamented:

> You have to educate customers and explain that the platform can help them reduce the cost of purchasing and enhance efficiency. You also need to educate investors because it is a new business, which is not as easy to understand as other

businesses like automobile manufacturing. This is the biggest bottleneck for me. I'm like a missionary, constantly pushing my projects to investors, so that they can understand what our company is doing in under five minutes.

In Congwei's view, China currently lacks the mature ecosystem for entrepreneurship present in other countries such as the USA. To better support these startups, he suggested that entrepreneurs be provided better access to support including talent and funding. In particular, he suggests that only companies that are responding to government initiatives or understand how to speak the language of investors can continue comfortably as entrepreneurs. This bottleneck is problematic as it tends to stifle truly novel and home-grown innovations that lie outside the purview of hot topics and industries. There may also be ethical ramifications, as Congwei highlights:

I think it will distract entrepreneurs. The entrepreneur must lower his head and do things that go against his outlook on the world, life, and values. I think it may not be a good thing.

Other executives also highlighted the risk and potential waste involved with allowing government incentives to drive innovation. As an example of this, Nicolas Musy, a Swiss national and founder of The Swiss Centers China and China Integrated, pointed to how there was initially a watch factory built by the government in every Chinese province, but ultimately only one survived because these were not being fueled by bottom-up innovation and diversification. He suggested that in the current environment,

a lot of people are only looking at how they can get subsidies rather than how to innovate .... The government is putting out so much money that the money becomes the target rather than the result.

In this way, China has largely taken a top-down method of innovation that relies heavily on government investment in certain technologies and industries. Nicolas believes that this approach has resulted in mixed results to date. As evidence, he pointed to the mandate in the 1980s and 1990s for multinational car companies to set up joint ventures with local companies to produce cars in the country. Although ostensibly the goal of this policy was for the local companies to absorb knowledge and learn how to produce their own cars, still today less than 40% of car purchases in China are of domestic brands. In response to this slow uptake, the government then decided to switched directions and invest heavily in electric cars. Even in this sector, the foreign company, Tesla, maintains the largest market share. Nicolas sees top-down methods of innovation to be less effective than bottom-up because it is difficult for a single company to have the highest levels of quality in terms of each of the individual components. He points to the Dutch semiconductor industry as an example of how sophisticated industries require an entire network of high-quality suppliers:

> There is a Dutch company making a machine that is used for producing last generation semiconductors. Each machine costs one hundred million US dollars. There is only one company in the world that produces this machine, and this machine is available only every three or four years. To build this machine, you need hundreds of suppliers who have themselves reach a very high level of technology, I don't think you can generate that just by pouring money into it. It's difficult to create a complete ecosystem for that level of sophistication.

Our interviewees opined that this approach can be particularly wasteful when these initiatives are not aligned with current market demand. One Chinese executive we spoke to share a clear example of this from their personal experience:

> I did two or three such projects in 2012 and 2013 .... We worked hard on those projects, but the market did not give positive response. As a result, our partners went bankrupt, and that business was ruled out. Almost ten years later, suddenly this market has begun to thrive. This failure cannot be ascribed to our innovative technology or

our past partners, but to the immature market environ-
ment. Innovation requires the right time, the right place,
and the right people.

EDUCATION AND CONTINUOUS LEARNING

As many interviewees highlighted in the previous chapter, high standards for education are critical for fostering innovation and creativity. Although China boasts some of the most competitive universities in the world, our research also unveiled some ways that education is currently transitioning in a way that mirrors their shift from a manufacturing-heavy economy to one of cutting-edge goods and services. Traditionally, education was used to reinforce cultural axioms of equality, discipline, hard work, and to ensure generalized standards of basic education across a huge nation. As most people would generally only be expected to follow instructions and meet design specifications in factories, critical and divergent thinking were not highly prioritized in mainstream education.

Alongside the shifting needs of the workforce, however, we note that several educational facets are also changing. Sometimes this happens proactively on the part of individual families through enrollment in specialized schools or the contracting of private tutors to help give students an advantage or a different perspective from others. Sometimes, this innovative mindset is sparked by an innate curiosity in the young people themselves. For example, Daniel Wang, the Director of the eLab at CEIBS in Shanghai, credits part of his success as an entrepreneur to the new perspectives he gained by befriending international classmates at a young age. In describing how he and his diverse friends enriched each other's' thinking, he noted that although Chinese students are more task-oriented and driven to identify effective solutions quickly, many Westerners take more time to truly understand the problem before taking action. To illustrate this idea, he points to the inception of the short-term home rental company, Airbnb. He recounted:

*There was a presidential election in Washington D.C.
and so many people flew in that they could not find
enough hotels. Airbnb solved the problem by using people's homes temporarily .... In China, people might have
started to build hotels years before in anticipation of this
influx of people.*

The difference in Western innovative thinking, in his view, is
recognizing that the issue is not a shortage of hotels, but rather the
inability to respond to temporary surges in demand for beds during
infrequent events.

A similar example can be found in Amazon's development of
its Web Services sector. Like the temporary spike in hotel demand
during the election, Amazon experiences a 10,000-fold increase
in website traffic during their annual Black Friday sales event.
Although they created the servers to handle this extra capacity,
they did not stop once they found the solution to their problem.
Instead, they pushed themselves to think how they might leverage
this new resource on the other 364 days when this extra computing
power was not needed. Hence, Amazon Web Services was created
to provide cloud services to a broader audience.

Exposure to diverse ideas over the years has inspired young
entrepreneurs like Daniel to ensure that he is viewing issues from
all angles (e.g., identifying the real problem in the Airbnb case)
before jumping to brainstorming solutions. Education aimed at
fostering innovation should teach people to look at problems in
new ways rather than focusing on the notion that one singularly
superior solution exists.

Several people we spoke to had additional ideas for how the
Chinese education system – particularly in the early years – might
continue to evolve to foster more innovative ways of thinking and
ensure preparedness for the dynamic workforce they are set to
join. Some, like Martin from Denmark, suggested a more student-
focused and less academically rigorous curriculum at young ages.
This would free up time for more diverse experiences, including
more self-reliance. Martin advocates for

*more free time and more unsupervised time to have rela-
tionships with their peers or simply go about entertaining*

*themselves and sort of pursuing what they find to be
meaningful at whatever age they are.*

Mats from Sweden agreed that much can be gained from letting
"children be children."

Releasing some of the unilateral pressure on academic competition could help students identify passions, build confidence, and gain
exposure to new ideas that fuel innovation. Building on this idea,
Roy from KnoHao cautions Chinese parents from using newfound
wealth to overly spoil children or shield them from even though most
minor of hardships. He contended that "the most important thing
parents can do is to be a role model. Teach children the importance
of hard work, of being independent, and ensuring they become self-
reliant." In doing so, they will be less afraid of taking risks and will
become more resilient, which can be useful for developing innovative
solutions to problems that do not have a single right answer. Another
Chinese manager echoed the importance of more social support for
failure that helps to foster innovative mindsets. They opined,

> *there are 100 reasons for failure while success entails all
> the conditions in place. We must realize that innovation is
> a long-term thing, as is venture capital. We need to set psy-
> chological anticipation and be more tolerant towards error.*

Part of this educational reform should be targeted at reconnect-
ing students with what makes them passionate, according to Roy
from KnoHao. He shared with us that when Chinese executives
visit Israel, they often remark on the marked difference in passion
they observe between the two nations. This is extremely useful in
the context of entrepreneurship and innovation as it motivates people to challenge existing ideas and come up with better ones. He
connects fostering this attribute early in life with making the most
of educational opportunities:

> *If the kid goes into university with much more passion
> to want to do something they want to do and that they
> find interesting, this will translate into a much more self-
> reliant graduate, someone who's much better at critical
> thinking and what we call innovation, particularly dis-
> ruptive innovation.*

Still, Roy cautioned that too much passion and individualism can have critical downsides in terms of innovation. For example, he admitted that

> *Israeli companies do an extremely poor job to scale up. They do a good job in starting up companies that have 10, 30, or 50 people. But huge companies, there are very few in Israel .... If you want to build a big company, you need some form of hierarchy. When you have many people with too much passion in a large company, that's also not going to be done so well.*

Encouragingly, there is some evidence that educational reforms in China are moving in this direction. In 2021, the government passed sweeping reforms to severely limit extra-curricular tutoring outside of school hours[14] and increase programs to boost student participation in sports.[15] In addition, some private schools in China are reforming education to be more well-rounded and unstructured, focusing on the Four C's of creativity, communication, collaboration, and critical thinking. Still, not all of this is in the hands of the education systems or the government, but often comes down to family life and the child's own personal choices and passions. Roy noted that training in self-reliance "must start in the home at age three. That's not the government's role, by the way." He is adamant that for China to make the shift from incremental innovation to disruptive innovation, imagination and play must be fostered within the family from a young age. Martin added succinctly that it is not solely either the government or family's responsibility, but "at the end of the day, it's also very much up to the individual."

OPENNESS DOMESTIC AND TO THE WORLD

Mirroring our discussion about innovation clusters in other parts of other world in the previous chapter, an examination of China's historical development reveals that it, too, developed different industries in specific geographic locations. The cities on the Eastern seaboard were among the first to be developed, with Shanghai serving as the financial center and Beijing the government head-quarters of the country. From there, Guangdong had the country's first major factories, Shenzhen became the epicenter of the technology industry, and Tianjin had a portion of the aerospace industry. As with the USA and other parts of the world, certain cities became synonymous with a given industry. There are two primary differences, however. First, these clusters were largely planned and dictated by government policies. Second, and perhaps more crucially, because of China's hukou system,[16] people are unable to easily move from one region to another, preventing the cross-pollination of ideas. Cameron elaborated on the problems this presents in terms of innovation:

> *I can take my family out of Seattle. I can move them to Kansas City or Wichita and the kids can go to school, we can integrate there, we can buy another house with no issue, and there are no restrictions or limitations. Whereas in China, if I move from Shanghai to Guangzhou for my work or my wife's work, we must worry about where we're going to live, where the kids are going to go to school, are they even going to be able to get into a good school because of the restrictions on the number of spaces available to children from outside the local area? As a result, what you see in China is that there are clusters of people that don't move.*

To help foster exposure to new ideas and new ways of working, making it easier for people to relocate from one part of the country to another would be a good start. Building on this, it would help to allow people to make more choices for themselves and allow them to pursue their passions. Kenneth from 3M sees many parallels between his company's culture and the most innovative nations in the world. He suggests that any country hoping to boost innovation should aim to gradually instill an environment that focuses on respect, patience, commitment, and the provision of ample resources. He reflects, "I believe this is really that simple. You must give people a free hand. You must be patient. You have to respect people's contribution."

Another key recommendation that surfaced during our research was one of the two key drivers of INSEAD's Global Innovation Index: an emphasis on open economy. In our conversations, the importance of further integration with the world, open access to information, and the international cross-pollination of ideas was viewed as a crucial factor for future innovation. As one example, Omar Al-Busaidy from the UAE – another nation that has developed rapidly in the past few decades thanks to astute government policies – suggested that building a loyal population base by meeting the peoples' needs and providing an ecosystem of prosperity is much more conducive to innovation than tight censorship of ideas and ways of thinking. Referencing his own country, he noted that whereas he understands the threat of being exposed to fake news or another country's negative propaganda:

> *We see a lot of news articles about the UAE that are clearly negative. Nobody is naive to the fact that certain activities are being carried out. However, when you block access to this information, sometimes you are giving the idea to not just your local population, but to the rest of the world, that you have something to hide. So, for me, I feel that with China there's still so much growth and so much they can learn by opening up even more now, but without necessarily feeling the fear that maybe by opening up it's going to corrupt their own people. If you're providing the love and care to your people, no amount of any kind of information will sway me or anyone away from the love of their country.*

With the dramatic positive strides that China has made toward prosperity and the swelling pride among citizens for their country, Chinese people are likely to feel the same. By allowing people to share ideas freely without repercussions and have open access to different ways of thinking, we contend that innovation – and particularly disruptive innovation – is likely to explode.

Enabling more international exchanges and access to information might also help to resolve another of the biggest barriers to innovation that many of our interviewees identified: the lack of understanding between the West and China. With greater exposure and exchanges, these misunderstandings are likely to reduce over time. It is also critical that we come together to do this. As Cameron noted:

> You must innovate to solve the world's big problems – global warming, not having food, poverty – there's a whole list of issues. How do we do that? We actually have to work together, innovate, solve, innovate again, work the problem, and innovate again. And the only way we're going to do that is by doing it together.

With the world's largest population standing to suffer at the hands of these grave issues, it would behoove China to work together with the world, and greater openness would help. Cameron elaborated further on why temporary measures like the great internet firewall are impermanent solutions and impede innovation in the meantime.

> Barriers have never worked in the history of humanity. The Great Wall didn't stop the Mongols from coming into China. The Berlin Wall didn't stop people from fleeing and within a generation it fell. These kinds of barriers we're now seeing with technology walls will pass at some point. At the moment it's largely a US and China issue. And this will absolutely be a challenge for a long time. But as we continue to innovate, as we continue to move forward, you cannot innovate if you don't work with and understand others.

Many interviewees reiterated that for true innovation to occur, there needs to be more cooperation and fewer 'us versus them' mindsets.

Although this works on a national level, it is also true of individual companies. To be a truly global organization and to take the best of ideas from all over the world is the goal of most firms that dream big. Cameron provided the following successful example:

Why is Tesla in China? Because it's using Chinese inno-
vation, manufacturing knowhow, expertise, and batteries.
That's why it's here. It must be here because this is the best
place in the world for that industry. If you are a Chinese
company doing financials, you have to be at some point in
New York or London.

Mats from Sweden also shared an eye-opening experience in
that recently he noticed that the exchange of ideas about innovation had become an equitable two-way street between Sweden and
China. He recalls a recent seminar where:

Swedish and Chinese scientists sat down and on the same
level, it was a true exchange in both directions of ideas.
I think we have come to a point where we are now truly
beginning to complement each other. One cannot say that
one is on a higher level than the other. We can all say that
we are coming from different parts. We need each other.
We need to draw the best from each side. Together, we
integrated ideas to create a new kind of sustainable bat-
tery production.

This raises the important point that for truly productive
exchanges to occur, other nations and companies must also offer
the respect and listen openly to the ideas and methodologies offered
by Chinese experts, even if different from their own.

To summarize, we conclude that China has done a remarkable
job in not only growing and evolving its economy and introducing
groundbreaking innovations to the world but doing these things
in a unique way that deviates from the traditional playbook. We
expect that China will continue its path to become a superpower
and world leader in innovation and will best be served by continu-
ing to create a new definition of what it means to be innovative.
At the same time, however, the best innovations do not occur in a
vacuum. As David from Buhler noted:

China and America, they need each other. They both have a
large-sized population and a huge economy, which allows

opportunity. Both have good universities. Both countries have very smart people.

The key for Chinese innovation, then, is that although a core focus on developing its own strengths and ecosystems is important, many of the best ideas for the future will come from being open, learning from others, thinking flexibly, and adapting the very best ideas from around the world to the local context. This concluding point was perhaps best expressed by Cameron:

> *When you look at innovation, you have to innovate together to be truly innovative. If you're only innovating by yourself, somebody is always going to come along and kick your butt because they'll be learning from other people, in other places, being able to integrate it and move it forward faster than you are. The more diversity of ideas you have, the better off you are, period.*

CONCLUSION

This chapter provided an in-depth look at modern-day Chinese innovation. We covered historical and cultural factors that have influenced innovation in China. The world could benefit from following China's example of rapid iteration to innovate more quickly and cheaply, particularly when facing tough competition. Although Chinese innovation continues to face significant obstacles, we believe that greater access to information, more cross-border exchange of ideas, and new modes of education can help to propel innovation in the country to even greater heights.

LEARNING POINTS

History of Innovation in China

China has a rich history of innovation that has continued to evolve over the millennia: from great inventions in the past, to economic reform, to manufacturing, and now to leading business model and technology innovations.

Innovation in Today's China

China has developed its own definition and method of innovation, which features rapid speed, iterative changes, and market responsiveness. The modern business environment is best described as one of fierce competition and breakneck speed. This is led by mostly by Chinese private companies. Characteristics of innovation in China are incremental, react quickly to market feedback, fast followers, and fierce competition.

Disruptively Innovative Chinese Companies

China is currently leading innovation in several industries, including EVs, FinTech, and business model innovations. There is a strong entrepreneurial spirit fostered by government plans and incentives.

Challenges Facing Innovation in China

Key challenges facing Chinese innovation include heightened pressure for environmental sustainability, slowed economic growth, limited access to capital for private companies, high-pressure education systems, and decreasing openness to the world.

Education and Openness

Best practices that may help China overcome these barriers include greater information and openness (both within China and between China and the world) and new education models that incorporate the freedom to pursue passions and new ideas. The education system should be more student-focused and include more diverse experiences by emphasizing the Four C's: creativity, communication, collaboration, and critical thinking. Society should be much more open, allowing domestic talent to move freely and exchange idea with the world at large. China needs to further integrate with the world, open access to information, and encourage international cross-pollination of ideas to become even more innovative.

NOTES

1. https://knowledge.insead.edu/entrepreneurship-innovation/global-innovation-index-2930

2. https://china.usc.edu/sites/default/files/forums/Chinese%20 Inventions.pdf

3. https://www.worldbank.org/en/country/china/overview#3

4. https://www.thinkchina.sg/construction-singapore-model-mainland-china

5. https://www.sciencedirect.com/science/article/pii/S1755309119300437

6. https://www.scmp.com/economy/china-economy/article/3045053/ china-cements-communist-partys-role-top-its-soes-should

7. https://www.ft.com/content/ad97c282-7b6d-11e0-ae56-00144feabdc0

8. https://www.statista.com/statistics/255778/number-of-active-wechat-messenger-accounts/

9. https://www.cnbc.com/2021/08/30/china-tech-crackdown-experts-warn-on-the-risks-ahead-for-stocks.html

10. https://www.ey.com/en_gl/ey-global-fintech-adoption-index

11. https://technode.com/2021/08/12/luckin-founders-new-noodle-shop-is-no-luckin/

12. https://www.sustainalytics.com/esg-research/resource/investors-esg-blog/how-china-s-electric-vehicle-(ev)-policies-have-shaped-the-ev-market

13. https://cbmjournal.biomedcentral.com/articles/10.1186/s13021-019-0130-z

14. https://www.caixinglobal.com/2021-07-26/china-spells-out-sweeping-reforms-to-turn-after-school-tutors-into-non-profits-101745804.html

15. https://www.bloomberg.com/news/articles/2021-08-06/china-sees-sports-as-growth-driver-after-its-olympics-success

16. The hukou system is a household registration system in China that identifies people as permanent residents of a given city. People are able to get social services and healthcare in their area of residence and the system strictly controls internal migration. Often, organizations must sponsor individuals to change their hukou.

4

THE IMPACT OF THE GOVERNMENT ON INNOVATION IN CHINA AND THE WORLD

Governments cannot adapt fast enough. That's a main challenge. Globally, governments cannot adapt or change fast enough to realize that everything's different now post-COVID. And a lot of that has to do with innovation and the acceleration of a lot of different things. I think what you will see is further global integration and further disintegration of institutions and the old way of doing things.

– Cameron Johnson, Partner at Tidalwave Solutions

INTRODUCTION

In reviewing the history and modern business landscape of innovative countries, it is evident that the governing people and institutions have an outsized influence on whether companies and
individuals are motivated and rewarded enough to pursue innovation. Our subject matter experts each recounted the key decisions
and policies that shaped their nations' orientation toward innovation. Government influence was also confirmed by the *2019 Global
Competitiveness Report* published by the World Economic Forum.
Following an in-depth analysis, they concluded that many of the
countries we profile in this book are among the world's highest
performing nations. For example, Singapore ranked #1, the USA
ranked #2, Switzerland #5, Sweden #8, Denmark #10, South Korea
#13, Israel #20, the UAE #25, and China #28. In terms of indi-
vidual facets, the USA ranked highest in business dynamism, Israel
had the most entrepreneurial culture, and Singapore ranked highest in interaction and diversity of people. To compile these scores,
the researchers assessed each country based on how enabling the
environment is for business, how healthy and skilled the human
capital is, how strong the markets are, and how robust the innovation ecosystems are. Government policies and procedures play a
role in each step of this process, from setting the tax rates to making educational policies to streamlining the process of registering
patents and safeguarding the legality of work contracts.

In this chapter, we will investigate each of our focal countries
in depth to determine how specific government actions, laws,
and policies have either shaped the culture of the country in the
past or help to attract top talent in the modern era. Some of our
profiled nations can point to the decisions of a few key leaders
that dramatically altered the course of the country's evolution.
Others point to present-day laws that create an ecosystem that
is favorable to innovation and entrepreneurship across a wide
range of industries. Although there is no one type of government
or a singular blueprint for country development that works in all
instances, we hope that the insights gleaned here help to showcase
a few key features that can help foster a nation that is fertile for
innovation.

Table 4.1. Focal Country Comparison.

Country	2020 Population (Millions)	Size (km²)	2020 GDP (in USD Billions)	Founding Year	Government Involvement
China	1,402	9,596,960	14,720	1949	High
USA	329.5	9,833,517	20,940	1776	Low
South Korea	51.78	99,720	1,631	1948	High
Sweden	10.35	450,296	537.6	1905	Medium
UAE	9.89	83,600	421.1	1971	High
Israel	9.22	21,937	402	1948	Medium
Switzerland	8.64	41,277	748	1848	Low
Denmark	5.83	43,094	355.2	1889	Medium
Singapore	5.69	719	340	1965	High

Source: www.wikipedia.org

The countries in this chapter are organized into three groups:

1. *Large countries*: the USA and China.

2. *Small and medium-sized countries*: South Korea, Sweden, Switzerland, Denmark, and Israel.

3. *Young countries*: the UAE and Singapore.

In Table 4.1, we provide a snapshot comparing various countries in this chapter (the countries are ordered by population size).

LARGE COUNTRIES

USA: A Partner, Not A Parent

In the USA today, the relationship between the government and organizations is often portrayed as more of a negotiable partnership rather than like a parent and child. This means that although the government does little outside of funding universities and think tanks to guide the specific direction of innovation, they can offer certain tax benefits or relax zoning regulations when it is in their best interests to do so. Thus, the role of the US government in relation to innovation is to make the business environment more attractive.

This wasn't always the case, as Cameron Johnson of Tidalwave Solutions reminds us. For many years, the government's Export–Import Bank was set up to arrange financing for US exports. Companies like Boeing relied heavily on this financial support to purchase machinery and refurbish planes. Although this financing has since dried up,[1] historically this was one way that the government helped to keep businesses afloat that needed access to very large sums of money (even when sales were not brisk). Cameron views the current laissez-faire attitude of the US government when it comes to directly funding or incentivizing cutting-edge research efforts and new production methods that can benefit society to be a key limitation of the country's current approach to innovation. This is because, he said, "generally, private industry is driven by making money, and is not necessarily altruistic or 'help my fellow man' motives, although I would argue it's changing a little bit now."

Omar Al-Busaidy, an Emirati who is currently working in the USA at the UAE consulate, also pointed to other areas that the US government can improve when it comes to innovation. Namely, he suggested that the government should work harder to innovate within its own systems and replace some of the legacy processes that have been in place for decades. He opined that

> the US needs to digitize very, very quickly … I can still look on their websites and things are missing. I don't think that they were very quick with going online and creating apps for services. The first thing that should be digitized and streamlined is the national ID. I don't understand why the national ID doesn't have everything in it – driver's license, passport details, and tax-payer ID. Also, why is the Social Security card paper?

A key obstacle to government change and innovation, he recognizes, are increasing geopolitical tensions and the lack of bipartisanship inherent in the country's increasingly polarized two-party system. In contrast to the rapid decision-making that is possible in countries like the UAE and China, the current system in the USA often stalls quick progress because every matter becomes a partisan issue that results in lengthy infighting.

There are other interesting – and indirect – ways that the US government shapes innovation. Outside of giving preferential tax treatment to corporate giants like Amazon, Tesla, and Boeing, local and state taxes can also have a huge impact on the multitudes of workers needed to drive R&D and develop new technologies. A prime example of this can be found in the costs faced by an engineer moving to a job in Silicon Valley. Cameron elaborates on this ancillary impact of government further:

> In California, if you look at the tax rate just in general, many individuals generally pay over 50 percent of their income just in taxes. If you add all of them up, as a software engineer in Silicon Valley making 200 grand a year, not only are you losing half your income, but you can't afford to buy a home so you probably don't live close to where you work, and there's all of sorts of additional costs that add up. In contrast, when you go to Texas or Seattle or Miami, you don't have all those taxes.

Extrapolated to a large scale of an organization, companies like Tesla are increasingly exercising their rights to relocate to other, more tax-friendly parts of the country to make it more attractive for their workers. This has been aggravated in recent years because the subpar public schools and large homeless population mean that many Californian citizens do not believe that the services they get in return for their taxes are equitable. With the rise of remote work during the COVID-19 pandemic, the value of facetime and physical proximity to other bright minds has also lost its luster. Thus, we see even more agency on the part of organizations and employees in that they simply relocate when the local government regulations become unfavorable. Federal government policies that allow freedom of movement across the country then serve to aid and empower both organizations and employees to pursue locations that are in their best interests, dispersing capital and talent for innovation to different geographical regions. This trend has also given rise to a certain element of competition between the individual states as well as new laws. For example, given the rise in employees buying homes in neighboring (and more tax friendly) states and commuting to work, many states are now trying to tax people based on where they work rather than where they reside. Cameron sees this is a shortsighted solution to a growing problem:

> *The states should instead look at it and say, 'OK, what are we missing here? How do we keep our talent? How do we make regulations more business and worker friendly? Because moving to Texas is not just about the taxes. It's also about fair business regulations. It's about actually having affordable housing for the employees and the staff. The medical costs are also cheaper than in California.*

Although it is a sticky quandary for the individual states, we believe that this mass exodus from historical clusters of innovation is likely to prove fruitful for the nation's innovation as a whole. Rather than centralizing the internet industry in Silicon Valley, for example, companies are now being spread into mini clusters throughout the USA. This dispersion is good not only for the cross-pollination and exposure to new ideas, but also lends itself to new sources of inspiration coming from varied physical environments. As Cameron illustrates:

> *Seattle is famous for the rain. Maybe someone moving there will think more about innovations for rain. Or if you're in Texas, maybe you think more about cows or horses. I think the different perspectives and environments will lead to newer innovations than would arise from a group of people who just want to go surfing outside their door (but there is nothing wrong with that!).*

China: *Centrally Planned Innovation*

Following an astounding era of economic development and modernization over the past 30 years, China is currently embarking on new transition to move away from manufacturing into innovation and sustainability. One way the government is guiding and reinforcing this transition is by regulating industries to increase quality and reduce waste. The government also has several policies in place that aim to create an environment that fosters innovation by buying technology, providing access to global markets through trade policies, offering financial incentives, building physical infrastructure, and enhancing the quality of talent through education.

Generally speaking, the Chinese government adopts a very centralized strategy for innovation, providing funds for very specific projects and initiatives it aims to prioritize. In this way, China champions a breed of "pull-style" innovation through government planning and funding whereas many other parts of the world adopt a "push-style" of innovation that results from consumer demands. Daniel Wang, the Director of the eLab at CEIBS, explains the motivation behind these targeted initiatives, suggesting that the incentivized industries and technologies are typically chosen because the government

> wants to catch up or aims to have a competitive advantage in certain areas. For example, take the automobile industry and electric vehicles. Around eight to ten years ago, the world was looking to move towards clean energy cars from petrochemical cars. At that time, the Chinese government gave a lot of incentives only in this industry.

These incentives then fuel the iterative and large-scale innovation strategy described in Chapter 3. Namely, although many of these funded companies and projects would fail or even be fraudulent, a handful of successful entrepreneurs will lead to demonstrable progress in these industries. As Daniel from the CEIBS eLab explains,

> the Chinese government invited companies like Tesla and all these big players in the global market to join and to co-work on a lot of the projects. For example, there is a car, Roewe, which is a car by the Shanghai Automobile Company that was co-created with a British brand MG Rover. Now, the Chinese new clean-energy cars are one of the biggest forces globally.[2]

In addition to the electric vehicle industry, similar incentive programs and five-year plans have been launched for microchips, artificial intelligence, and FinTech.

INNOVATION STORIES

Deng Xiaoping and the Transformation of China

Deng Xiaoping is considered the father of modern China. He took the reins of the country in 1978, two years after the death of Mao Zedong. He transformed China from one of the poorest countries in the world to a true world power. He didn't have a straightforward design to reform his country. One of his famous quotes summarized his experimental philosophy: "cross the river by feeling the stones." This process entails trying something, experimenting, improving on the original idea, and implementing it across the country. At a time in which the figure of Mao was still powerful, he said: "poverty is not socialism and to be rich is glorious." He was a courageous man who was very determined to make China prosperous.

He was the right leader in a time of uncertainty. He was convinced that there were things that China could learn from developed countries, even if they were quite different from China. For example, he once remarked that "it does not matter if a cat is black or white, so long as it catches mice."

During his leadership, China joined the web community, the World Bank, the International Monetary Fund, and later the WTO. He opened the country to foreign investment, which allowed China to learn from the more advanced economies in the world. He also promoted sending Chinese students to study abroad in the USA and Europe. His objective was clear, as he noted that "when our thousands of Chinese students return home, you will see how China will transform itself." His policies unleashed the energy and potential of the Chinese people.

Deng visited Singapore in 1978 just after he was appointed as the leader of China. This visit was crucial as he saw how Singapore prospered very rapidly under the leadership of Lee Kuan Yew, the Prime Minister. He understood that strong government and economic freedom were a very successful combination. Lee Kuan Yew was also very impressed by Deng Xiaoping. Lee Kuan Yew wrote about Deng Xiaoping in his memoirs The Singapore Story:

> He [Deng Xiaoping] was the most impressive leader I had met. He was a five-footer but a giant among men. At 74, when he was faced with an unpleasant truth, he was prepared to change his mind.

Source: Vogel, E. F. (2011). Deng Xiaoping and the transformation of China. Cambridge, MA: The Belknap Press of Harvard University Press.

These incentive systems are launched by the central government at a national level and passed down to the various regions to execute. These regions are also divided in terms of different focuses, with Shenzhen focusing on high-tech innovations, Suzhou developing electronics and computer chips, Shanghai serving as the economic center, and Ningbo excelling in exportation and advanced manufacturing. In contrast with some of the natural clusters that formed in places like the USA, Chinese clustering is more centrally directed by the government and often closely aligned with government incentives in these industries. This also filters down into the individual districts within cities. Daniel from CEIBS uses Shanghai as an example, noting that

> the incentives are more aligned with what they are trying to be as a center or as a region. For example, in Shanghai, Zhangjiang Hi-Tech Park is more for electronics and medical pharmaceutical companies, whereas if you are a financial company or if you're doing FinTech it's better to go to Lujiazui Financial Center. If you work in Lujiazui, the Huangpu government will give your company much more support and also all of your supply chain will be located there.

Martin Bech from Denmark points to the wind turbine sector that was originally led by state-owned enterprises, but now also includes several privately run companies as a prime example of "pull-style" innovation. Propelled by government support, this industry now has a number of prominent competitors for the large European wind turbine manufacturers. Importantly, although this has led to the emergence of a few giant innovative companies, there is still enough market share leftover for the fast-followers to be successful. Thus, until the middle class stabilizes and the markets come closer to saturation, there isn't much incentive or push for all companies to be innovative in order to survive. However, this is likely to change as more and more Chinese companies look to expand globally, which will require new methods and innovations than those that are successful in China.

One side effect of the "pull" model of innovation is that the resulting technology is often too prohibitively expensive to replicate in private companies or even by most other governments around the world. One example of this from China is the high-speed rail system. Although this effort began with contractors from international companies, there was a huge push to develop local technology and patents to create the highly efficient system that exists today. Martin noted that

> this is a fascinating success for China, but it's expensive. It costs such amounts of money that it's almost impossible for any other country to finance something similar. When these Chinese train manufacturers and railway constructors go out and try to sell themselves to other countries, it's very difficult to actually make a sale because of the cost of an infrastructure project of this kind.

To remedy this disconnect, Jonathan Woetzel from McKinsey recommends that hands-off settling periods should follow large government investments to ensure that these newly formed companies and industries are agile, affordable, and responsive to customer needs. As examples, he points to the necessary investments into planned cities and economic zones such as Shenzhen. He contended that although

the so-called organic development of cities is certainly,
generally speaking, a much more reliable model for the
development of economic competitiveness than the
planned approach, sometimes, one has to do the planned
approach in the absence of having a marketplace.

Following their conception, markets should be allowed to develop naturally and should evolve according to the needs of the local consumers in a trial-and-error approach to adapt to the local context.

Although the Chinese government has a more decisive role in the economy than many other countries, Cameron contended that true innovation in the country is increasingly being driven by the private sector. He opined that

that's where we see the high growth companies. That's
where we see the digital innovators. That's where we see
the global champions, generally speaking, is in the private
sector companies.

Within the private sector, he sees that most of China's innovation coming from customer demands (e.g., Internet companies), supply chain optimization (e.g., manufacturing plants), or new scientific and engineering breakthroughs (e.g., pharmaceuticals and semiconductors). As the home of such a huge consumer market, each of these innovation types can be scaled up tremendously, leading to a natural advantage.

Much of the private-industry innovation in goods and services has been targeted at serving the needs of a fast-growing middle class. As Mats Harborn from Sweden observed,

the Chinese middle class is now expecting that Chinese
products are at least as good as foreign products. And I
think that's putting a new kind of pressure on the Chinese
companies.

Daniel from CEIBS agreed, sharing that:

Around 2006 or 2007 we started to see more and more
consumer products in the market that had acceptable

prices and good quality. At that time, we had a more diverse array of products in stores on TaoBao and the versions of Chinese YouTube and Chinese sharing sites were just getting started. It was around that time that I noticed that the economy was switching from being very dependent on export manufacturing to trying to make better products based on manufacturing improvements, and also looking much more carefully at domestic consumption.

For multinational companies, this means that there is a shifting pressure to set up R&D capabilities in China to design products and services that meet the preferences of this unique consumer market. Several of our interviewees shared that often the products developed by these Chinese R&D teams are later launched in other markets around the world.

Another trend that is helping to fuel Chinese innovation is the re-patriation of citizens from around the globe. With the rise of opportunities in China, instability in many parts of the world, and swelling national pride, Chinese people are increasingly returning home after years of studying and working in foreign countries, taking the novel ideas and new perspectives they gained with them. Mats noted:

I see Chinese employees moving away from Sweden and European companies and going back to Chinese companies because they get more freedom in the Chinese companies. They have very quickly adapted to a new world with much more flat organizations, less hierarchy, more freedom, and more flexibility.

At the same time, the Chinese government has recently levied a series of educational reforms. These include a strong crackdown banning for-profit tutoring services and limiting tutoring on nights and weekends. In addition, the number of qualifying tests for elementary school students have been reduced. These changes are aimed at modernizing the education system while also reducing the pressure on students.[3] The government also wants to structure a more well-rounded experiences for students by increasing their involvement in sports and extra-curricular activities. Together, these trends are likely to enhance the innovative capabilities of Chinese citizens in the future.

Going forward, our experts agreed that China is on track to become more innovation-driven than ever before. This innovation will not be limited to the government-prioritized industries of finance, AI, and sustainable technologies. For example, China has begun to make notable strides in business model innovation, including using technology to make food delivery and shopping more convenient using mobile applications. We also see that the Chinese government, given the lack of legacy systems, is able to take more risks in terms of innovation than many Western countries. As an example of this, Cameron points to the launch of the new digital currency in the country. He observed that

> once the actual digital currency comes alive, it will be a game changer. It will change in everything we know about finance globally. And this is one way, again, that China will affect the world within this decade. You will see almost every major economy in the world have some form of digital currency. That's all because China's doing it first.

To accelerate innovation going forward, Jonathan from McKinsey called for more policy support for entrepreneurship to ensure that people are rewarded for taking risks. He elaborated:

> We need to continue to provide new and ever more powerful forms of infrastructure, along with the environment that supports entrepreneurship. Notably, a business friendly environment where it's possible to come to market fast and raise capital. Importantly, to provide incentives for innovators, which includes the ability to get a return on your capital and a return on your intellectual investment.

The government is also encouraging the big technology companies to use the huge amounts of data they control to solve social problems and fuel innovation. When asked to share the advice he had for future Chinese entrepreneurs, Cheng Hang,[4] the founder of

HUPU Media Company, said "I strongly recommend creating real value and solving other people's problems." Jonathan from McKinsey similarly observed that

> everybody has an innovation strategy. What differentiates innovators is that they actually innovate. They are able to invest in innovation …. It's this question of how to encourage risk taking and not just talk about innovation, but to actually do it.

Ultimately, our interviewees agreed that China is poised to grow exponentially in terms of innovation during its next stage of development. David Wang from Buhler opined that the modern entrepreneurial spirit of China's youth combined with strong and effective government efforts to accelerate economic growth will be the keys for future innovation. To augment this process, he suggested that society "let people with very strong mindsets, the free-thinkers, try new things and don't make them afraid to make mistakes." If these efforts are successful, he concluded that "China is on the fast lane of innovation and in the next ten years it will be a superpower. I have no doubt about that."

SMALL AND MEDIUM-SIZED COUNTRIES

Israel: *The Promised Land of Innovation*

One interesting factor about the impact of governments on innovation that we uncovered over the course of our research is that frequently laws and policies evolve over time as a country's needs change. A prime example of this is Israel. When the young country was first founded in 1948, it adopted a very centralized and socialist structure wherein many of its industries were owned and operated by the government. In the 1980s and 1990s, the government moved to more of a free market structure. Despite the small population, Roy Chason recounted that this opening up "led to a huge push of entrepreneurship, invention, and innovation in Israel that didn't exist so much in the previous decades." Because of the lack of natural resources and limited access to capital, fledging companies faced added pressure to create valuable products and services that appealed to international markets.

Today, the government of Israel continues to evolve and create new initiatives that help to fuel innovation. As evidence of this, Israel is a world leader in R&D investment, investing 2.7% of its GDP each year as compared to 2.7% in the USA and 2% in Europe.[5] They also claim 12.9% of the publications in the 10% most cited journals (as compared to 15.3% in the USA and 11.6% in Europe). Although a large portion of this investment comes from private companies, the government also plays a role through the Chief Scientist's Office. This arm of the government heads innovation initiatives and helps provide government funds to various startups. There are also government-funded incubators around the country that are increasingly more specialized into specific sectors such as agriculture and healthcare. In this way, there are many ways that the government helps to enrich the innovation ecosystem in the country.

INNOVATION STORIES

Military Unit 8200 and Innovation in Israel

The 8200 brigade is the most famous unit in the Israeli armed forces due the numerous startups created by former members. Its mission is to identify communication signals from foreign countries and identify those that might threaten the nation. Every Israeli, excluding certain minorities, must serve in the military for either 32 months (men) or 24 months (women). However, only the top high school students are selected and go through a very rigorous selection process to be chosen for the 8200 unit. Given the high level of selectivity and the demanding development the soldiers undergo, the members of the 8200 unit are in high demand by companies after completing their service. They often start their own companies using the experience and the knowledge gained during their time in the military. The 8200 unit has four important attributes that determine why so many former members can be found working in the country's high-tech sector[6]:

1. *Debrief.* It is customary that after every mission, the team reflects on what has happened, the lessons learned from where the team performed well, and the things that can be improved in future missions. During the debrief sessions, everybody is free to speak, and rank is not considered. The rules of the debrief sessions are open communication, an open flow of ideas, and equality.

2. *Continuous learning.* Another aspect of the unit culture is continuous learning. Rules and regulations can be challenged. Members of the unit are always looking for opportunities to improve.

3. *Flat hierarchy.* There are fewer senior leaders than in other military units. The flat hierarchy favors flexibility, initiative, and rapid decision-making.

4. *Networking.* Only the most competent young people are invited to join the unit. They work together for three years in challenging situations. This creates a strong bond among them and a sense of brotherhood.

As a final thought, the members of the unit assume significant responsibilities at a young age. They are under pressure, must make rapid decisions, and execute these decisions fast. All of these are ingredients that help to form successful entrepreneurs.

Sweden: *Symbiotic Ties for Design and Quality*

Sweden has a long history of fostering close ties with other nations to help foster innovation. Given the limited access to capital in the country, many entrepreneurs often form companies in other nations like the USA. As Mats from Scania shared with us,

> *young entrepreneurs went over to the US and found that we, as a young, very dynamic society, were solving problems in different ways. Later, they took their ideas back to*

Sweden, refined them, developed them, and then created new companies. One such example is Tetra Pack.

As a result of these close ties between the two nations, Minnesota today boasts a huge Swedish population and any new trend in the USA quickly becomes available in Sweden, underscoring the value of international idea exchange for innovation.

In terms of the priorities the Swedish government has for innovation, much of the focus since the oil crisis of the 1970s has been on sustainability and renewable energy. To foster innovation in this sector, the government declared that it would achieve negative emissions by 2045 and has introduced a series of tax incentives to help it achieve this goal. In additional, all the different siloes of the government are united toward reducing dependency on fossil fuels. This longstanding government priority has translated into demonstrable advances, including ranking the highest for biofuels per capita among the 23 member countries of IEA Bioenergy.[7]

Other Swedish industries that have historically benefited from government initiatives include the mobile industry and the development of fighter airplanes. Today, however, the government tends to play a more hands-off and tends to leave more of the onus on private firms. One exception to this policy can be found in the cooperation between the government and the country's universities. As Mats shared with us, there are many programs that firms can apply to get funding and an academic contact to conduct research and development projects.

Denmark: *Safety Nets Promote Risk Taking*

When discussing the role of the government, many of our experts cited the importance of having ample government support to meet peoples' basic needs. In Denmark, this support begins very early in the life cycle starting with early childhood education. As Martin from ATV Denmark explained, "the education system here is often credited with the capacity to problem solve or at least come up with new ideas, maybe doing two things at the same time." From there, the government also has a series of funding bodies where organizations can apply for financial support to help them develop new technologies and services. Today, the government is particularly interested in supporting the development of innovations related to sustainability. Outside of the government, there are also increasing amounts of venture capital firms in the country and there are also private foundations like the Novo Nordisk Foundation that incubates entrepreneurial projects to help bring them to market.

In addition, Denmark's labor laws mean that companies can easily hire and fire people, which gives firms more leeway to try new ventures and develop new technologies. The social security system also ensures that people will be taken care of if they do find themselves out of work. Although some argue that this leads to decreased proactivity and personal responsibility, it also allows individuals to take more entrepreneurial risks. "For those who are prone towards entrepreneurship, they can actually do a lot within this framework while still being on the safe side, not risking that everything will be taken from them because the state will provide for them if they end up in a bad place," Martin explained. Thus, one critical role that the government can play is to ensure that the education systems and social support are provided so that people are not so worried about their day-to-day survival that they become risk adverse.

South Korea: *Betting on One Horse at a Time*

It is impossible to design experiments with countries to measure the impact of governments on development. However, sometimes history gives us a glimpse of what these experiments might reveal. Take Korea as an example; North Korea is among the poorest countries in the world, whereas South Korea is among the richest. Clearly, government matters.

Although South Koreans enjoy nowadays a high per capital income, this was not the case only a few decades ago. In fact, after the Korean War (1950–1953), it was one of the poorest countries in the world. Even as late as the early 1960s, South Korea was primarily an agricultural economy that still heavily relied on American aid. How was this dramatic transformation possible? Aligned with Chapter 2, factors like history, prioritizing education, and cultural traditions of hard work and critical thinking contributed to this miracle. In addition, specific government initiatives also played a role. Considering the country's limited national resources and the small size of the domestic market, the Korean government launched the national innovation system (NIS)[8] to begin the country's rehabilitation. At each stage of development, the government focused on a single sector or priority rather than diversifying the economy. For example, the first five-year economic development plan was focused on job creation and less on innovation, and therefore prioritized labor-intensive industries like textiles and footwear. In the 1970's, the focus shifted to automobiles, shipbuilding, steel and other heavy industries. It was also during this time that the major Korean conglomerates, known as *chaebols*, were created. In the 1990's, high-tech became the priority, and innovation took a central role in this new stage of development as the government invested in the creation of industrial cities and science parks. The new focus on innovation also meant that the government cooperated increasingly with the private sector, research centers, and universities that led innovation efforts. Many of the largest Korean organizations today were born out of this collective effort, including Samsung, LG, and Hyundai.

Dr Tae-Yeol Kim, a Korean national and Organizational Behavior Professor at CEIBS, explained that:

> *Many Korean companies followed Samsung; they were the model for the rest and other big companies learned from Samsung. One of the things that Samsung did in the 1980s was to very actively recruit experts. They went to the US to recruit doctoral students. At the time, many Koreans went to US to pursue their studies. Samsung aggressively recruited them even one year before they went to the US. They hired many engineers, scientists, and managers. LG and other companies followed these kinds of practices. Nowadays, they also hire from other countries. If you go to the Samsung headquarters today, you will see many foreigners.*

In recent years, the Korean government moved away from the *chaebol* strategy to focus SMEs and entrepreneurship. Important current policies are:

1. The promotion of social networks of innovation through workshops, conferences, and seminars.

2. Changes of regulations to facilitate the creation of new ventures.

3. Research cooperation between industries and universities.

4. Promotion of global networks with countries like Singapore, Japan, and China in education, research, and industry.

These policies are helping the country to become an innovation leader, as South Korea appears 5th in the *Global Innovation Index 2021*, 5th in the *2020 Ranking on Doing Business*, and 8th in the *2020 World Digital Competitiveness Ranking*.

Switzerland: *Unity Through Diversity*

Switzerland, like many countries, is divided into regional factions called *cantons*. What is unique, however, is the autonomy enjoyed by each of these 26 cantons.[9] These regional-level governments each has its own legislature, constitution, and judicial systems and can therefore oversee many features of business and daily life including taxes, healthcare, and the police force. This unique government structure was established by Napoleon Bonaparte in the 1800s,[10] as he deemed the people from various regions to be too diverse and difficult to manage. By giving each region its own voice and the autonomy to control its internal affairs, he sought to impose cooperation by having the cantons work side-by-side in horizontal conferences when deciding federal issues.

Nicolas Musy, a Swiss national and the founder of China Integrated, shared that there is a slight element of competition between the cantons given that each can levy different tax levels at or above the unified minimum level of roughly 13%. This and other historical factors have led to a certain degree of localized specialization in different regions, similar to the clustering effects described in Chapter 2. For example, the Geneva area is very strong in life sciences, finance, and diplomacy. The Jura low mountains region is famous for precision-manufacturing of everything from watches to

CNC machines to semiconductors given its origins in watchmaking. St. Gallen is famous for all textile-related activities and Basel is known for its strong chemical and pharmaceutical industries. In addition, there are 10 major universities funded by the cantons, including the prestigious Lausanne and Zurich Institutes of Technology, which help to further fuel innovation. Finally, the structure of the canton system sets a precedent for grassroots governing that helps breed trust and cooperation. Nicolas elaborated further on the impacts of this bottom-up political structure by citing the example of referendums:

If you can gather a hundred thousand signatures on one issue, you can bring it to a vote at the country level where there is eight million people. It's a very low barrier for initiating political discourse. There is a lot of political debate ongoing at all the levels. You can bring an issue for a vote not only at the federal level, but at the cantonal level and also at your local level, the community level. This one condition creates enormous amounts of trust, which is the basis for cooperation. One of the key characteristics of Swiss innovation is a very dense and efficient ecosystem of very specialized small companies able to cooperate across many disciplines to develop new technologies and products.

There are several other ways that Nicolas believes that government policies have shaped innovation and accountability in Switzerland. For example, he described the policies surrounding the government funding of innovation, wherein for the most part the government will not finance companies' R&D directly. Instead, they frequently fund public–private projects for organizational technology development and prototyping. When organizations submit a proposal, they agree to fund a certain percentage of the project executed by the company while the government funds applied research carried out by a public research institution partnering in the project. The exception here is for basic research, which is funded by the government through the research universities. One missing aspect of the current funding structure, he noted, is that there is comparatively little seed financing available for startup companies. He observed that *it's quite limited when compared to China; I think that the highest amount you can get is around one hundred twenty thousand Swiss francs .... This is also what people say is one of the weaknesses of the innovation system in Switzerland. There is little angel money and there is also not the same access to capital as compared to the US.*

A final unique way that the Swiss government is aiming to fuel innovation is by establishing Innovation Centers at a number of its consulates around the world. As an official branch of the science arm of the government, this initiative was started to support Swiss startups that are operating in different parts of the globe. Its first outpost was set up in Boston and funded with private capital raised by a Secretary of State for Science & Education from Geneva. Following its success, the project was then expanded to Silicon Valley, Shanghai, Singapore, India, and Japan. These locations have physical space in the consulate so people can work and network, and they offer a variety of services to help connect Swiss entrepreneurs to new ideas and networks around the globe. One of these services is funding a trip for 10 Swiss startups to visit Shanghai each year. During these Chinese immersion experiences, the founders interact with local companies and meet with venture capital firms to explore opportunities in the region. In sum, there are both historical and structural factors that lead the government of Switzerland to incubate high levels of innovation.

YOUNG COUNTRIES

Singapore: *Strong Government and Business Freedom*

The fact that Singapore – a country smaller in size than New York City – has solidified its position as a preeminent world leader in innovation in just over five decades of history has captivated the world's attention. Much of this success can be attributed to forward-thinking leaders and strong government influence. As a city-state, "probably the biggest corporation in Singapore is Singapore itself," opined Hellmut Schutte, a German National and the

Former Dean of INSEAD at Singapore. Hellmut cites the vibrant ecosystem and detailed government policies as key drivers of Singapore's success. He shared that the

> *government considers itself to be at the service of their own people, and they are all extremely competent. I'm very often asked, "why is Singapore so successful?" My answer to this is very clear. It's the competence of the government. Full stop. I've now lived in Singapore for 20 years, and I have always had quite a lot of contact with government officials. I have not once met a government official who was not competent.*

Most of the government's policy decisions are levied via their Economic Development Board that sets targets and provides financial incentives for target industries such as biotechnology. The government has also established a number of think tanks that are consistently turning out new technology to transform things like IT systems and weather control and forecasting.

Given its small size, Singapore's strategy for growth and prosperity has heavily depended on attracting and cooperating with multinational organizations. Hellmut shared that the government is organized into roughly 20 divisions with around 300 people on average working in each to support industry, including multinational organizations. In contrast with the huge economies of the USA and China, Singapore only has a handful of local large companies (primarily focused in real estate and banking). One way the government attracts multinationals and foreign talent is by levying comparatively low-income taxes. Other government policies that help in this effort are maintaining English as an official business language, offering a stable currency, enforcing laws transparently, and creating an environment with lots of economic freedom. Hellmut shared that living in Singapore as a foreigner,

> *it's all very transparent and very easy to understand. I mean, if you cannot function as a foreigner in Singapore, you better stay in your village. Actually, it is probably easier to understand Singapore than your village.*

INNOVATION STORIES

Lee Kuan Yew – The Man that Created Singapore

Singapore became a colony of the British East India Company in 1819 and was occupied by the Japanese during World War II from 1942 to 1945. After that, it became a self-governed British colony. In 1963, Singapore became part of the Malaysian Federation. Due to racial conflicts, the Malaysian Parliament expelled Singapore from the Federation in 1965. It was a difficult time for Singapore. Singapore is a small island of 50 km (31 ml) by 27 km (17 ml). It does not have natural resources, had a low level of education, no military, no industries, and seemingly no future as an independent country. In contrast, today Singapore is one of the most innovative countries globally, a hub for international business, enjoys a low crime rate, and is one of the wealthiest countries in the world. How could this dramatic transformation be possible in such a short period of time?

The answer is Lee Kuan Yew (1923–2015). He was the prime minister of Singapore from 1959 to 1990. He is considered the founder of Singapore and the person that gave stability to the city-state. To enact this transformation, he created strict laws like the death penalty for drug trafficking, a very advantageous tax regime for foreign investors, and created the national military service program in 1968 with the assistance of Israel. He also established policies for integrating the three cultures that formed Singapore: Malays, Chinese, and Indians.

Lee Kuan Yew was a charismatic leader. His assertive communication style brought people together. He also had a powerful vision for his country as the business hub of Southeast Asia. Part of that vision was to make Singapore a corruption-free government. Strict law was part of it, but also having well-paid and educated officials. Education was another objective. Singapore has six autonomous universities and ten foreign institutions, including INSEAD, St. Gallen, and the German Institute of Science and Technology. The fantastic development of Singapore and its continued success cannot be understood without Lee Kuan Yew's leadership.

Sources: Britannica, T. E. (2018, September). *Lee Kuan Yew: Primer Minister of Singapore.*

Retrieved from Britannica: https://www.britannica.com/biography/Lee-Kuan-Yew; *How did Singapore become such an advanced economy in such a short time?* (2016, February). Retrieved from Quora: https://www.quora.com/How-did-Singapore-become-such-an-advanced-economy-in-such-a-short-time

UAE: *If You Build It, They Will Come*

Purpose and ideology are what drive the initiatives and strategies pursued by the Leader of Dubai and the Vice President of the UAE, Sheikh Mohammed bin Rashed. Namely, he is not motivated purely by personal legacy, but rather views himself and his government as responsible for reinvigorating the greatness of the Arab world. As our Emirati interviewee, Omar, described:

> *When it comes to innovation, he [Mohammed bin Rashed] talks about places like Mesopotamia, Babylon, and Damascus, and how the West used to go to these places to learn. This was the golden era for this region and everybody used to come and they studied and innovated from here. A lot of different concepts came from this region, and I feel like Mohammed bin Rashed is trying to recreate that. He's become a beacon of hope to contrast the kind of stuff that usually makes headlines in the Middle East. He wants to change that narrative for the region; he wants to rewrite history from being called the Middle East to the Modern East.*

One of the strategies the government is using to harken back to the golden era of Arabian history is by making headlines for the right reasons. Dubai is world-renowned for its seemingly endless list of architectural marvels, including the world's tallest building (Burj Khalifa), the world's tallest hotel (Gevora Hotel), the largest mall (which includes the largest aquarium in a mall – The Dubai Mall), man-made islands, and, most recently, the world's deepest pool at a depth of 200 feet.[11] These feats are not merely the flashy accessories of a cash-rich nation, according to Omar, but instead deliberate investments on the part of the government to act as a cradle for innovation and to signal to the world that its people are competitive and poised for success. Once again, he credits history for the inspiration to pursue this strategy, noting that:

> This is something that we learned from other empires before. If you look at the Romans, you look at the Greeks, what made them stand out? They were all about infra-structure. You cannot be a successful or iconic as a country or an economy if you don't have massive buildings that people can recognize and identify your country by. We didn't have anything. Nobody is going to come here and be excited to see a tent in the middle of the desert. But everybody wants to come and see the tallest building in the world.

Once the distinctive buildings and other attractions put Dubai on the map, existing brands and companies were attracted to come and add to the melting pot of nationalities, companies, and ideas that is the modern UAE. By following the example of Singapore, the UAE government sought to encourage this diversity by making the environment attractive and by providing incentives so that citizens and non-citizens can live together in harmony. Chief among these was not charging income or sales tax initially. The government is also very quick to adapt policies if they notice that people are starting to leave the country. Omar shares the example of visa renewal:

> Before you had to renew work visas every two years. Then they saw it was starting to annoy people and they saw

that people were leaving the country. They said, OK, fine, now we'll make it every three years. And this made people happy. Now there's the 10-year golden visa. This is a good example of how the government adjusts their policies agilely to keep people happy but also generate money.

By creating an attractive environment that brought the world's ideas and investments into the country, the government was able to ensure high levels of diversity and unique perspectives that later contributed not only to Emirati innovation, but also to the growth of transient residents and companies. Reflecting on the region's history as a transient hub for knowledge and innovation, the current government leadership is aiming to brand the UAE as a springboard where people can start their businesses and careers before growing them and bringing their knowledge elsewhere. Citing a recent interview with the UAE Minister of Economy, Omar said that

if Israel is the Startup Nation, then the UAE is the Scalable Nation. That's what everybody has been able to do, businesses, people, etc. They were able to come to the UAE first and then they scale from the UAE and then they end up in places like China.

As an example of one initiative aiming to bring this philosophy to life, the UAE government is currently sponsoring the education of one million Arab coders from across the region. Although a small percentage will settle in the UAE, the goal is that the vast majority return to their countries to develop their own economies. In addition, home-grown companies like Nakheel (a real-estate company) and Emaar (a telecommunications company) are now expanding their footprint to countries around the world.

Sheikh Mohammed's general guiding philosophy when structuring Dubai's government's policies and practices is to run the government like a company. As an example, after observing how digital solutions helped private companies to offer increasing convenience, he was inspired to enable citizens to access government services at any time. Rather than facing long lines and filling out paperwork in government offices, most of the services and applications can be completed online or through mobile applications. Although this innovative government strategy has been in place for several years, the COVID-19 pandemic in 2019 accelerated many of these plans to reduce unnecessary social interactions.

Another aspect of running the government like a business is to lean on a strong core of advisors on the Dubai Economic Council. This group of people represents the country's major merchants that collectively make up around 40% of the UAE's GDP. By listening to the needs and ideas provided by local business leaders, the government is able to be more responsive to the changing needs of the various industries.

CONCLUSION

There are many interesting ways that the large countries, small and medium countries, and young countries are similar and different from one another in terms of government intervention. Although all of the countries in this chapter have consistently been named among the world's most innovative, we can see that there is a large degree of variability in terms of how planned or organic this innovation has been. Even within a given category, we can see that this diversity abounds. For example, the governments of the world's two largest economies – the USA and China – have used vastly different approaches to fuel innovation. Part of this can be attributed to the overall ages of the countries we sampled. Regardless of size, many of the countries that found themselves comparatively less developed than their peers in the mid-1900s seemed to have benefited from targeted innovation initiatives and strong government oversight that has helped them to "catch-up" to the mature economies in record time. Clear examples of this can be found in the youngest nations we profiled, Singapore and the UAE, but also in the incredible transformation that China has experienced over the last several decades. Early examples of these government interventions are creating policies and laws that make their nation attractive for foreign investment.

This is not to say there are no differences in strategies between the countries of different sizes, however. As compared to the larger economies, which can dabble in innovation across a variety of industries, we see that the small and medium-sized countries tend to specialize into only a handful of industries. In this way, they are able to build up suppliers and a level of detail and quality that helps them to survive among the giants. We also see that these nations share a number of cultural characteristics, including a tradition of hard work and a government emphasis on education.

As a final point, many of our interviewees underscored the challenges that are presented by a post-COVID world. As the chapter's opening quote illustrates, some suggested that the undeniable interdependency of the world's economies and supply chains means that global innovations are needed to prepare for future disruptions like those caused by the pandemic. Roy also echoed the point that as we reemerge to a dramatically changed world, the lessons of the past and of other successful governments may be limited in their applicability. He pointed to his home country of Israel to illustrate this point:

> You cannot change or emulate your historical DNA. For other countries to try to copy the Israeli model on that historical angle it is not possible. But you can learn from the geopolitical and the government policies, and you can also try to emulate some of the features of modern society and culture into your corporate organization or to your company's environment.

LEARNING POINTS

Governments and institutions have an outsized influence on whether companies and individuals are motivated and rewarded to pursue innovation.

Large Countries

Government support for innovation in the USA largely comes in the form of tax incentives and creating affordable and business-friendly environments to entice companies and employees. The main role of the USA is to provide the right environment through laws, education, and competent administration. There is also a high degree of internal competition among states and high mobility of businesses and people within the country.

China champions a breed of "pull-style" innovations through government planning and funding whereas many other parts of the world adopt a "push-style" innovation that results from consumer demands. The government pursues five-year plans in which innovation is of high priority. In contrast with other nations, there is reduced mobility of people and businesses across provinces. Chinese returnees play an important role in the development of the country.

Small and Medium-sized Countries

Although the government continues to devote considerable resources to research and development, *Israel* provides a model for how countries can move from a centralized and strong government control to market-led innovation. Modern-day Israel has a thriving private sector that is very connected with the military and a mature venture capital market.

Sweden, which is world-renowned for its high-quality products and minimalist design, has been shaped by government policies focused on ensuring sustainability following the oil crisis of the 1970s. There is a close connection between Sweden and the USA and strong cooperation between the Swedish government and universities.

Denmark makes extensive investments in education to help groom innovative citizens. There are ample social services that free citizens to pursue entrepreneurship and innovation without fearing for their livelihoods. There is also a flexible labor market that gives companies allows companies to quickly adjust their employee number and try new ventures.

South Korea is perhaps one of the best examples of governments offering support for highly specific innovation sectors (e.g., high tech) to help grow the country's economy very rapidly. The government plays a central role in the different states of growth, from job intensive industries after the Korean war, to big conglomerates, to high-tech giants and entrepreneurship nowadays.

The diverse cantons of *Switzerland* help to fuel healthy internal competition, regional specializations in innovation, and horizontal cooperation. Famous areas of innovation include the precision manufacturing industry in Lausanne and Geneve and research in Zurich and Basel. Today, Switzerland provides a very stable business environment thanks in large part to their efficient government.

Young Countries

Singapore's development can be traced back to highly competent government officials, who are highly educated and well-paid. Its model is based on attracting top international companies and enforcing strict, yet transparent and fair, local laws to maintain stability. There are also low taxes and flexible regulations for companies.

Innovation in the *UAE* is mission-driven as it aims to be a symbol of reinvigoration of the Arab World. To accomplish this goal, local leaders have invested heavily in infrastructure and unique architectural achievements to attract top talent and multinational companies. They also offer welcoming regulations for businesses and favorable tax rates for residents.

NOTES

1. https://www.aier.org/article/kill-the-boeing-bank-once-and-for-all/

2. https://www.cnbc.com/2021/04/02/chinese-electric-car-start-ups-nio-xpeng-post-strong-march-deliveries.html

3. https://internationaleducation.gov.au/international-network/china/PolicyUpdates-China/Pages/China%27s-education-modernisation-plan-towards-2035-.aspx

4. https://www.ceibs.edu/video-podcast/21157

5. https://www.eolasmagazine.ie/why-israel-leads-the-way-in-rd/

6. https://www.ntegra.com/insights/israel-start-nation

7. https://www.ieabioenergy.com/wp-content/uploads/2018/10/
CountryReport2018_Sweden_final.pdf

8. Mazzarol, T. (2012). *Building a national innovation system: What can we learnt from Korea?* The University of Western Australia. Retrieved from https://theconversation.com/building-a-national-innovation-system-what-can-we-learn-from-korea-9449

9. https://www.worldatlas.com/articles/the-cantons-of-switzerland.html

10. https://www.swissinfo.ch/eng/swiss-celebrate-napoleon-s-historic-act/3174096

11. https://www.cnbc.com/2021/07/13/dubai-opens-a-200-foot-deep-pool-with-an-underwater-sunken-city-.html

Section II

ORGANIZATIONS THAT ARE INNOVATIVE TO THE CORE

In the second section of this book, we drilled down to better understand the various components of an innovative organization. Our research on this topic began in 2020, when we launched a survey and collected responses from 950 executives across a variety of industries to assess their attitudes and current practices on innovation.[1] When asked to rank order features of an innovative climate, 55% said that continuous experimentation was most important, whereas 52% selected quickly responding to customer needs, 36% selected clearly communicating the organization's values and principles, and 35% selected decision-making based on data. These factors have also been highlighted by external sources, with the Boston Consulting Group's (BCG) 2021 Most Innovative Companies Report noting that innovation leaders differentiate themselves from innovation laggards by defining a clear ambition, outlining innovation domains, rewarding innovative performance, empowering agile teams to tackle tough projects, and creating a culture that attracts top talent.

Our primary goal in this section is to illustrate that imbuing a culture of innovation is not a surface-level, quick-fix, but rather involves multiple mutually reinforcing factors. Organizations that can establish the correct values, create the right policies, practices, and leadership norms, and manage the right types of talent are characterized as true innovators. About cultural values, we believe that deeply innovative organizations are characterized by environments that champion *safety* (i.e., encouraging intelligent mistakes), *openness* (i.e., the capacity to break up organizational silos), and *diversity* (i.e., the celebration of differences). It is also critical that these values are reinforced at every level of the organization by attracting the right types of people to work for you, leading them according to servant and entrepreneurial leadership principles, and rewarding them through agile organizational practices and policies. To conclude this section, we paint a roadmap of how organizations can embark on a cultural transformation with the goal of implementing innovation at the very core of who they are and how they operate.

We used three surveys for as background information for Section II (Fig. II.1):

1. The 2021 Innovation Survey published by the China Europe International Business School (CEIBS). CEIBS is the number one business school in China and is consistently among the top ten in the world according to the Financial Times ranking. The Innovation Survey was conducted by the three authors of this book.

2. Most Innovative Companies 2021: Overcoming the Innovation Readiness Gap published by BCG. BCG is the second largest consulting firm in the world by revenue. Its headquarters are in Boston, USA. To gain a deeper understanding of this research project, we interviewed Ramon Baeza, a managing director and senior partner at BCG and one of the authors of this report.

3. The Adaptive Learning Organization Research Report published by NIIT, a global information technology learning provider and talent development firm headquartered in in Gurgaon, India. We interviewed Kamal Dhuper,[2] who is currently the President of NIIT China.

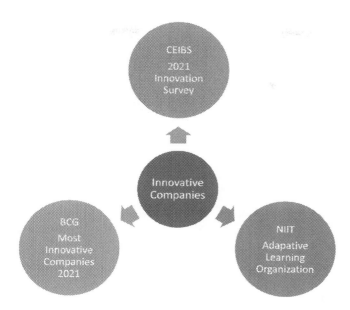

Source: Authors' original work.

Fig. II.1.   Most Innovative Company Sources.

These sources have been incorporated into the following chapters in Section II. The model that emerged from our interviews is depicted on the following page in our model.

INNOVATIVE TO THE CORE MODEL

Innovative leaders must ensure that all aspects are in place simultaneously for innovation to occur. Thus, it is better to envision each mutually reinforcing component of innovative organizations as part of a system rather than a step-by-step hierarchy. This is represented by this model of concentric circles in which each ring supports the inner layers and operates as a whole. Each element of the model will be developed in the subsequent chapter in Section II.

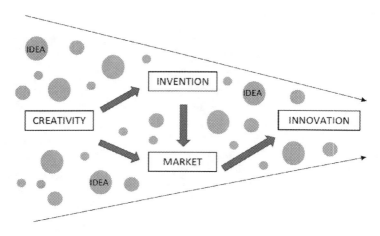

Fig. II.2. The Funnel Model of Innovation.

Each of the five chapters in this section will reflect one step in our Innovation to the Core Model. The last chapter will focus on how organizations can make the transformation from a traditional company to one that is innovative to the core.

The interviewees for this section include experts from a wide variety of industries, nationalities, and positions from organizations from different parts of the world.

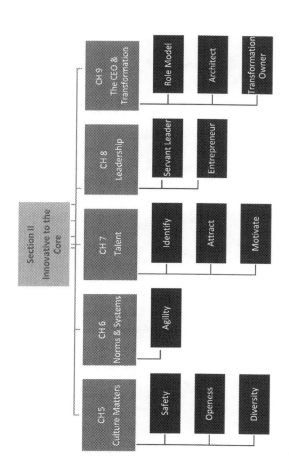

Source: Authors' original work.

Fig. II.3.   Section II Structure.

NOTES

1. https://www.ceibs.edu/sites/ceibs.sit.site1.drupalagile.com/files/import_files/sites/default/files/research/reports/others/2021-innovation-survey-report-en.pdf

2. We have six video interviews with select industry executives that are available for viewing on the website of the first author (www.juanleadership.com).

5

CULTURE MATTERS

They took away my fear of making mistakes. I learned that if I make a mistake, I will not be punished for it. And this makes me focus not on being afraid of my boss, but on taking care of the needs of my customers.

– Jari Grosse-Ruyken, Managing Partner of hivetime, quoting an employee of the Chinese restaurant chain, Haidilao

INTRODUCTION

As organizational behavior scholars, the bulk of our research centers on identifying how organizations can build ecosystems that are most fertile for innovation. In our experience, many companies tend to take a superficial approach to becoming an innovative organization, opting to tweak the mission statement or redecorate the head office without checking to see whether the leader behaviors and corporate policies are reflective of the new focus on innovation. Although some of the organizations featured in this section of the book have grown organically into innovation powerhouses based on the early values and culture set by the founders, others have been successful in orchestrating a true cultural shift from efficiency and hierarchy to innovation and the easy flow of ideas. Still others are still early in their innovation journey. This illustrates that although there is no one single formula (or timeline) for creating an innovative organization, there are certain elements that these organizations have in common that allow them to capitalize on and implement novel ideas more effectively than their competitors. Importantly, these factors involve more than simply agilely adapting the external environment or hiring brilliant minds. At the root of a fundamentally innovative organization is establishing the right organizational values that serve as the scaffolding upon which the corporate culture is draped. In this chapter, we highlight several examples of companies doing an exemplary job of championing the core values of innovation: *psychological safety, open* communication about new opportunities and ways of work, and embracing *diversity*.

CREATE AN ORGANIZATIONAL CULTURE THAT VALUES INNOVATION

In business schools, we preach a consistent refrain that the organizational culture must be aligned with the strategic objectives of the company. If you want to compete on costs, strict procedural regulations aimed at enhancing efficiency and strong management oversight are critical. If you want to be more innovative, there needs to be more agility and freedom in both the policies and the communication among employees. Despite this broad stroke advice, we sought to better understand the underlying values and priorities that can be distilled from organizational cultures that are innovative to the core.

Many of the entrepreneurs and founders that we interviewed anchored their organizational cultures on their own personal beliefs about how to get the most out of their employees. Another common theme, however, was that there should also be enough flexibility in the system so that the diverse values and priorities of employees can also be celebrated and supported. As an example, Cheng Hang, the founder of the sports platform HUPU, outright rejected the notion that employees should be forced to adhere to the mission, values, and vision of top leadership. He questioned, "if every person is unique, that means the company's mission will never fit other people in a company besides the founders." To remedy this, he decided against selecting a few narrow objectives to force upon his people, instead opting to build the company culture around empowering people to pursue their own passions and visions. Taking this to the extreme, he allows individuals with entrepreneurial ideas the opportunity to pitch their new projects and spinoff their own satellite companies, establishing their own culture, values, and mission in the process. Citing Peter Drucker,[1] he takes the philosophical stance that the whole of society's resources should be devoted to enabling entrepreneurship and that innovation should be normalized in everyday life. He has imprinted this viewpoint on his own corporate culture, sharing that:

> Every time I interview young men or women, I look at them and ask how can this young girl or young boy become an entrepreneur in five or ten years? I tell them when I hire them, "I am your lower limit. Your bar is where I am right now. You've got to be better than me in the future." And that's actually happened. Mr. Yang was the second member in Shenzhen when we started in 2004. Today, he runs a company much, much bigger than HUPU that has over ten thousand employees.

By empowering employees to pursue the projects that they find most meaningful (and allowing them complete autonomy once they spinoff into a new organization), employees retain their passion and are motivated to innovate given that the potential rewards of having their own company are so great. In this way, the organizational culture champions openness to ideas that is reinforced by financial support for the new ventures within the mother organization.

The importance of a strong and supportive organizational culture was cited time and time again by our interviewees. In fact, some, like Mats Harborn, the President of Scania China, noted that once employees experience working for an open and collaborative company culture, they often find themselves unable to adapt to other companies that enforce rigid hierarchies and a single way of doing things. Often, these employees will come back to work for companies with more innovative cultures even after leaving for a time in pursuit of more competitive salaries. Many emphasized that the allure of feeling respected regardless of your title and being able to take calculated risks without being punished are critical for attracting and retaining top talent that drive innovation. In all, we found that empowering and respecting employees was a core tenet of the most innovative corporate cultures we reviewed.

To become innovative to the core, it is critical that organizations establish and reinforce a principle-based mission. A famous example of a company culture that energizes its organization through a shared purpose is Apple.[2] In particular, younger people want to work for companies that have an impact on the world; money is no longer a key motivator nor the central purpose of top creative jobs. Apple's mission is to deliver the best products in the world and to leave the world a better place.[3] Managers bring this shared purpose alive by giving employees examples of out they make an impact: their stores provide training and assistance to anyone who needs it, their user-friendly products help older generations connect more easily with family and friends in the digital world, and disadvantaged youth are encouraged to learn the language of tomorrow through coding workshops. When employees feel that they are part of a community that is making a difference in the world, they will be motivated to derive truly innovative solutions.

In the sections that follow, we drill-down into the three most important core values that make up these cultural perceptions.

PROMOTE PSYCHOLOGICAL SAFETY

One core cultural value for innovation is a concept called psychological safety. Coined by Harvard professor Amy Edmonson, this entails creating a work environment where one feels free to go against the group's or leader's opinions, share half-baked ideas, and make mistakes without fearing punishment or social repercussions.[4] Frequently, this is manifested in the leader's attitudes about failure. The reason that this is so critical for innovation is because very rarely are first ideas and attempts successful; they require iterations and experimentations to perfect. In fact, recent studies have shown that the first few ideas generated during brainstorming sessions are often the least creative.[5] In innovation hubs like Silicon Valley, you see this wisdom adopted almost as a battle cry, with companies like Facebook pushing their employees to "move fast and break things." Kern Peng, a Lab Head at Intel in the USA, echoes the importance of tolerating failure, sharing that employees in his organization are expected to "fail fast and fail forward."

In contrast, a recognition of the importance of failure has also been slower to evolve in other parts of the world. As an example, Martin Bech, an advisor in the Danish Academy of Technical Sciences (ATV), notes that in his home country of Denmark people have traditionally been culturally reticent to fail. Despite this fact, innovation has been traditionally incubated within companies that:

> Deliberately create very secure environments. Here, there is a sense of security and a sense of possibility to contribute that leads people to try to see if their idea can fly with their colleagues, can be taken up by their colleagues, and they try to develop new things and not be very worried about the consequences, because it's a decision that may be strategic or tactical.

These organizational culture perceptions are fueled by very flat organizational hierarchies, high levels of interpersonal trust, and low power distance. Combined, these factors allow employees in many innovative Danish companies – even those at low levels – to feel safe enough to engage in candid conversations with their colleagues and supervisors about new ideas for products and services. To encourage more innovation outside the confines of these safe zones, the country is now attempting to spread the message that failure should not be feared more broadly in society. This has been particularly important in "impact" entrepreneurship, where people are so determined to solve sustainability problems that they are willing to risk the occasional failure along the way.

INNOVATION STORIES

Innovation Requires Patience at Cargill by Jerry Liu

About 20 years ago, we developed a sugar reduction solution. One of the key ingredients is chrysotile, a zero-calorie sweetener. It's organic. It is fermented from corn-based products with zero calories. Cargill developed it about 20 years ago. The demand for this new product 20 years ago was weak, so it never really took off. However, last year in China, one single company drove the demand for this product and we suddenly become part of their supply chain. The zero calories sugar took 20 years to reach the market. Not many companies or shareholders have the patience to wait this long. Cargill has a long-term horizon with regard to innovation.

I'll give you another extreme example: Cargill is also working on sustainability. Around the same time, Cargill developed a new product, which is degradable plastic for packaging. It comes from corn and is a packaging material. Cargill was losing money with this product, but recently it took off. They talk about carbon neutral, and there's great demand. Cargill truly believes in its values and puts the money behind their words. We care about our mission, which is helping people to live in a healthy way. It is always a top priority of both the shareholders and management, and we are not afraid to hold onto innovations until the market is ready.

Kern Peng notes that many traditional Asian companies typically have a lower tolerance for failure. "If they invest in it," he observes, "they want to see results." Cameron Johnson, a Partner at Tidalwave Solutions, also sees traditional Chinese business culture – where openly challenging one's superiors is unheard of – to be a stifling factor for innovation. In addition to reinforcing strong hierarchical power structures, taking risks and spending time to think creatively have traditionally been discouraged. Instead, employees are expected to use their work hours purely for task execution. Though these norms were nearly universal in the past, Cameron sees changes in many organizations as the younger generation brings management ideas back from their time working and studying abroad. Thus, particularly in younger companies, there is now much more fluidity in decision making and cultural norms are enforced to try and eliminate the importance of hierarchy from the minds of employees. He predicts that once those from younger generations become "directors and senior managers of companies, they will likely allow some flexibility and uniqueness while still maintaining a Chinese way of doing things."

Martin from Denmark already sees these trends unfolding in many of the Chinese technology companies and entrepreneurial ventures lead by this cohort. He observes that

> they are also coming up with ways of organizing new companies around new technologies that will probably present themselves as alternative ways of organizing compared to what is there already. I think some of the younger entrepreneurs in China are trying to tread a different path.

Once again echoing the value of a hybrid push–pull approach to innovation, the younger generation has been able to leverage their global exposure and incorporate Chinese elements to create their own methods of innovation. A good example of this is the internet company Bytedance, which does not assign job titles for its employees and their employee numbers are randomly generated rather than reflective of their tenure with the company. This serves to break down the psychological walls between the younger and more mature employees, helping to reinforce the idea that anyone is free to bring up new ideas or opinions.

Examples of other Asian companies that have mastered this blended approach abound. Jari Grosse-Ruyken, the Managing Partner of the Shanghai-based consulting group hivetime, shares several notable cases. As one, he points to DBS, a Singaporean bank that has become one of the most successful and customer-centric banks in the Asia Pacific region. To achieve this respected status, they first leveraged their localized knowledge of what Asian clients value and delivered this better than the established international banks. Second, they did not require that all employees in the organization focus on innovation. Although innovative cultures and practices are emphasized at the top levels of the organization, the lower levels are still managed in a very autocratic way, to the point that they are given verbal scripts to use during client interactions. Although typical Western organizations assume that this level of mechanistic control eliminates customer-centricity, it works in East Asia because the minority at the top of the organization does their research, debates with one another, and collectively comes up with the best ideas that are then executed by the masses.

According to Jerry Liu, the China President of the food and agricultural company Cargill, this rise in entrepreneurial spirit in China among the young and highly educated is being driven by a fierce hunger for success and a willingness to work incredibly hard. In contrast with many European and American companies, there is less of an emphasis on work–life balance and relaxation. Because of the long work hours, this leads to a cycle of innovation that proceeds at an incredibly rapid place. Moreover, competition for multinationals is stiff given that Chinese consumers are much more flexible when it comes to accepting new brands as compared to more mature markets in Japan, the USA, and Europe. Thus, innovation in this sector must be accelerated, and reducing innovation responsibility to a few key players at the top of the organization is one way to stay competitive in such a fast-paced environment.

Sometimes, however, this easily scalable model of customer service innovation falls short in terms of perceived authenticity. As an example, Jari describes how all employees at Family Mart convenience stores wear uniforms, greet the customer in an identical manner, and maintain uniform standards of cleanliness and decoration. Though superficially friendly, it can appear a bit robotic. To truly get to the highest levels of personalization and enthusiasm in customer service, he notes that empowerment and creating safe environments where employees are free from the fear of making mistakes is critical. As a successful example of this, he points to the popular hotpot restaurant chain, HeiDiLao. Despite most of the servers lacking a college education and hailing from rural provinces in China, service is consistently excellent with employees smiling and joking with the customers and immediately resolving any issues that arise. When Jari asked a server recently why they were so different from the competition, they proudly replied with the opening quote from this chapter.

Still, it is important to note that the enthusiasm surrounding cultures that push people to fail quickly to gain a competitive edge has waned as of late.[6] In the modern era, its critics warn that large-scale collaboration and measured exploration are more viable methods for creating innovations that will be too big for any one enterprise to overtake. Xiaolin Yuan, the President and CEO of Asia Pacific for Volvo Cars, thinks that this more calculated method of failure – which he dubs "intelligent failure" – is likely to be more fruitful than reckless experimentation. He notes that rather than creating a culture where all failures are good, organizations should allow risk-taking that is aligned with clear business priorities. In this way:

> If you have a real business case with a clear plan of how to do it, with the capability and resources to do it, to me, even if you later fail, at least you've learned something. But if you blindly say "we have a culture to try, and we don't care if we fail, it's worth it no matter what because if we succeed it will be amazing," that's a waste, and that's poisonous.

He opined that this is particularly true for large, established companies that must consider their reputation in the broader market. Rather than blindly chasing every new trend or opportunity, risk-taking should be controlled, measured, and aligned with strategic goals.

FOSTER OPENESS

Aside from creating a safe space where employees do not fear failure and are able to take developmental risks, a second core cultural value that we found to be driving the most innovative organizations is a sense of openness and collaboration. Our interviewees emphasized that this can be manifested both in the physical space of the office and in the communication norms among employees. Open communication fuels creativity because employees benefit from peer feedback and are exposed to new ways of thinking that can spark further iterative innovation. Perhaps the most straightforward in expressing the importance of this virtue is Zhenping Zheng, a supervisor at Openex Intelligent Technology company in China. He shared that in his company, they

> seldomly use the word "innovation," instead, "open" is more frequently used in our company. As you can see, the English name of the company includes the word "open," and we mean it. To us, openness means being willing to entertain new ideas, new projects, or new customers while searching for business opportunities.

For the benefits of an open mindset to accrue, however, employees must be encouraged to have the courage to speak up and share the ideas that they have about how things might be optimized.

To signal the importance of collaboration and promote social interactions, many organizations alter the design of the physical office environment. This may involve having gathering places like food hubs in the center of the office, tearing down walls, and reducing physical signs of hierarchy such as premium office locations and prominent title plaques. In addition, it may entail having perks and design elements that appeal to a large array of people. Kern Peng from Intel pointed to Google as the stereotypical example of this approach. He observed that to boost creativity, Google employs individuals who are not only experts in software programming, but are also artists and musicians. However, he noted, *if you are an artist and you go into a traditional company with grey-colored walls and carpets, it's dull and industrial looking. Do you think artists enjoy that working environment? No, they go in there, and they feel uncomfortable. Your office design essentially pushes people out.*

As employees tend to draw conclusions quickly about whether they fit into the new organization or not, these early impressions based on the physical environment can be critical. Thus, to ensure that you are encouraging the types of behaviors aligned with the company strategy, it is important to consider the details of your office design and perks. Kern offered the example of game choices in the company breakroom: sports-based games like foosball may be better for fostering competition, but strategy-based games like chess may be better for deep thinking and contemplation.

Though open-planned workspaces and enhanced perks are becoming more and more commonplace in organizations that aspire to be innovative, Jari warns that these can sometimes lead to counterproductive distraction. Aligned with recent research touting the benefits of blocking "Do Not Disturb" time chunks throughout the week for heightened productivity,[7] he recommends creating rules around certain key times when casual chitchat in the common areas is not allowed. This helps to create a healthy balance between ideation and refinement, because he shares,

more often than not, innovative ideas come from people focusing. And you can't focus when you are disturbed by your colleague every 10 minutes asking for help with this or that. I really think that many of the easy fixes that are being discussed currently and are not really well-designed to further the goal of innovation.

Aligned with this point, we emphasize that superficial efforts to boost innovation will be likely to fail if they are not paired with a careful consideration of the types of behaviors that these – and the accompanying policies and leadership tactics – will ultimately foster in employees.

Beyond encouraging mere exposure to coworkers via the redesign of office spaces, many of our interviewees suggested that organizations should take deliberate measures to eliminate organizational silos and encourage cross-departmental collaboration. By maintaining a fragmented organization where only top leaders of each function are allowed to converse with one another, employees become pigeonholed in their own function's way of thinking and priorities. As a result, the natural infighting and failure to consider the perspectives of others prevents people from coming up with solutions that are truly beneficial for the organization. According to Kamal Dhuper, the China CEO of the Indian conglomerate, NIIT, part of this can be accomplished by adopting flexible and adaptive policies that can be changed along with the environment. By emphasizing the importance of continuous learning rather than blindly following rules, employees will feel freer to reach out to others across the organization to understand diverse ways of looking at the same problem. Freeing lines of communication across levels of the organization is imperative, he notes, because "many times, new ideas come from the people at the front lines because they are in touch with the environment, competitors, and customers." In many traditional companies, there are barriers stopping low-level employees from engaging with top-level decision makers. In a learning organization, however, the priority is on identifying and acting on new insights, regardless of where they originate. Innovation is most likely to occur when people feel energized and connected behind the singular purpose of learning and growing to help the organization succeed and when this enthusiasm is unhindered by needless bureaucratic regulations and norms.

Of course, like many features of deeply embedded innovation, this cross-pollination of ideas is often easier said than done. Congwei Huang, the founder of the Chinese company Z-trip, acknowledges that his biggest obstacle as he continues to scale up his company is avoiding the natural congregation of employees into siloes. As he notes, "when there are more and more employees in the company, they may naturally gather into groups based on common interests, and the organizational structure will gradually become rigid." To try and counter this momentum, he has implemented several policies to help employees connect with and act on their own passions, rather than getting bogged down by conformity and climbing a prescribed corporate latter.

INNOVATION STORIES

Long-term Innovation at Intel by Kern Peng

Intel was founded in the second half of 1968 and by 1969 they already began to turn a profit. Until now, there has only been one year that they lost money in 1986. Obviously, all companies go up and down. No company can continuously be doing great things all the time. Intel has an excellent financial record. Intel has transformed itself many times. At the beginning, Intel was primarily doing computer memory. A lot of people probably still think Intel is a PC company and say that the PC is going to be replaced by mobile technology. However, Intel is not just a PC company. Intel's biggest profit, and our gross margin is close to 60%, is coming from the Xeon processors, data centers, and cloud computing. On the one side of Intel there are PCs, and on the other side it's the server market.

How is Intel transitioning into different businesses? It's because of Intel's culture. Intel has some bureaucracy because all large companies that get to a certain point, they need it. They must have certain processes for control. But overall, it's a very open management system. Our decisions are typically made at the lowest level possible. Part of the Intel culture is talent stability and new talent acquisition. Intel has a lot of people that have worked at Intel for a very long time and is also constantly hiring new college graduates. Intel very seldom hires people that have been working in another company for several years and then come to Intel. We like to train our own people. That's why it doesn't matter if the

> economy is in a downturn, Intel never stops hiring new college graduates. When they come in, we train them. Over time, the devotion of these long-term employees helps us to pivot the fundamentals of Intel's culture into new and innovative products and industries.

HIRE FOR DIVERSITY

A third and final cultural value that acts as a key ingredient for innovation is diversity. By diversity, we mean not only embracing demographic and cultural differences, but also different professions, educational backgrounds, personalities, and ways of thinking. By ensuring that there is a mix of ideas and perspectives, employees will be able to avoid tunnel-vision and groupthink that can occur in homogenous groups. Diversity also leads to more innovative ideas and solutions as people share and debate their different ways of viewing a given issue. If you know you will have to defend you ideas from someone who thinks differently, you will do extra research to ensure that you've done your due diligence. In this way, diversity can aid innovation by avoiding the creation of surface-level thinking and echo chambers.

Supporting the importance of diversity, some countries have used diverse talent to enhance the development and creativity of their nations as a whole. According to Omar Al Busaidy, a Fulbright scholar and economic affairs intern at the UAE consulate in the USA, the founder of the UAE, Sheikh Zayed Al Nahyan, convinced the various Emirates to come together as a single nation, living by the mantra that ten fingers together are stronger than five. Although this notion of unity through diversity originally referred to the seven local regions of the country, this philosophy was soon extrapolated to include welcoming residents from foreign lands to reside and contribute to the country's development. Diversity was also an inherent part of the UAE's history because people from around the world were constantly passing through their trade ports to exchange wares for the city's famous pearls. Recognizing that they lacked the human capital to achieve their goals of rapid development, they soon began offering incentives for highly skilled educators, healthcare workers, and businesspeople to live and work in the country temporarily. The local leaders were open to sharing their newfound prosperity with foreign residents because of the belief that the land and all its resources – including oil – belonged to God and not to any one group of people. Together, these historical events and the beliefs of the country's founders resulted in a national attitude of openness and belonging. Importantly, they did not just offer jobs to diverse individuals, but took deliberate steps to ensure that their nation was welcoming and accepting of all beliefs and lifestyle choices. For example, though the UAE is a Muslim country based on Islamic values, they had laws in place to allow foreign people to drink alcohol in bars since the country's founding. Once these diverse people were living harmoniously together in the same small country, progress and innovation occurred rapidly. This growth ultimately culminating in Dubai's current reputation of *madinat alhayaa*, which means the "city of life" in Arabic.

Although our interviewees unanimously agreed on the importance of diversity, they differed somewhat in terms of which type of diversity is most valued in their organizations. For example, one Product Manager for a prominent Chinese technology company contended that teams should be structured like a spectrum with each team member occupying a unique frequency. They further shared that

> *each individual is unique, and I see gaps among employees. This gap could be the result of experience, knowledge, education, or family background, and these differences can sometimes be difficult to manage. Nevertheless, I appreciate the inclusion and diversity, I think a team should be filled with distinct experiences and backgrounds.*

Jerry from Cargill also pointed to several innovative products that were implemented following the appointment of several senior managers who were women. Acknowledging the creative benefits of adding fresh perspectives to the team of people who make strategic decisions, he sagely noted that:

Sometimes, the success of a company in the past will be a barrier to being successful in the future because you live under the influence of the past. You leverage what you learned in the past, and that's not good enough for you to deal with the future. A lot of times we must learn from the competition, the same industry, from customers, from suppliers. We can get best practices from other companies. Relying on yourself is not enough, because you will be limited by your own experience.

Instead of making all decisions according to your own inherently limited past experience, he advocates hiring people from different industries, countries, and genders to help to provide new insights that can fuel company innovation going forward.

As with most good things, however, too much diversity can have its downsides. The Shanghai-based German consultant, Jari, noted that "diversity, especially cognitive diversity, is extremely difficult to manage." Although he agrees that diversity has a clear link to creativity and innovation, he suggested that it is important that organizations have the capacity to endure the additional time that it takes for diverse teams to become cohesive and for managers to learn how to manage each unique employee.

The importance of being open-minded and learning from diverse others was emphasized by Jonathan Woetzel, a Senior Partner at McKinsey, and Director of the McKinsey Global Institute. He shared with us that MBAs from top US business schools have become a distinct minority in his consulting firm in recent years. To complement people with this traditional background, they now hire more engineers, scientists, and athletes. To leverage these unique insights, he concluded that the most important factor is to ensure that the organization fosters

a unique learning environment for people from whatever background and hopefully we live up to that challenge of helping them develop that potential and to put it to good use in as many ways as we possibly can.

Of note, some interviewees suggested that diversity is only needed for certain types of innovation. Roy Chason, the Israeli founder of the company KnoHao, suggested that although incremental innovation (i.e., continuous improvement of products and services) can be attained with a homogenous workforce, disruptive innovation (i.e., creating something completely new that has never existed) requires the collaborative work of diverse employees. He elaborated that this is because

> *people see things and come with knowledge from different parts of the world or different functional areas or different social classes or men or women in a very different way. It's only when you combine those different perspectives together that you can create something out of nothing.*

He suggested that countries with comparatively small percentages of foreigners such as China or Japan might consider allowing more diverse voices to join in the creative and decision-making processes in companies to create truly disruptive innovations.

Kern Peng, a Lab Head from Intel, also cited a low tolerance for diversity among traditional companies in China as a key barrier for innovation. He observed,

> *in China, a lot of people in these companies all come from a similar background and similar situations, even the engineers they hire come from similar schools and have had similar training. In Silicon Valley, however, you have engineers that come from all different backgrounds and all different schools.*

Even within the same culture, some schools may emphasize theory more and others practical application, leading to divergent ways of problem solving. By having employees interact and learn to work with people from different cultures, professions, and educational backgrounds, firms that prioritize diversity as a cultural pillar have the potential to make products that are relevant for consumers around the world.

In addition to the wisdom of seasoned executives, the importance of diversity for creativity and innovation is backed by scientific research. For example, studies have shown that working in heterogenous, interdependent groups lead to greater individual innovation[8] and that cognitive diversity leads to team and individual creativity when employees adopt a strong learning orientation.[9] As alluded to above, it is also important to note that diversity is not simply an exercise in diverse hiring. In order to gain innovation benefits from a diverse workforce, organizations must have first effectively instilled the first two values that we discussed. That is, only in psychologically safe environments will people feel comfortable sharing their diverse perspectives and opinions, and only in open environments will this exchange of ideas even occur.

Citing his own survey conducted at Boston Consulting Group, MG and Senior Partner Ramon Baeza noted that companies in the Top 50 of the BCG Innovation Index tend to have comparatively high levels of diversity in their leadership teams on average. Importantly, he echoed our contention that it is important that this diversity is valued and well-managed for it to result in innovation. As recommendations in this regard, he said that companies should aim to ensure that everyone's opinions are heard, create environments where employees feel safe to propose new ideas, empower employees to make decisions, share credit for successes, give timely and specific feedback, and make broad changes based on suggestions. In addition, Cameron Johnson, a Partner of Tidalwave Solutions, suggested that regional hubs should not be rigidly separated from one another, but instead should be allowed to intermingle and move. Although it is natural for divergent preferences and ways of thinking to evolve in different geographical regions (e.g., the European outlook and culture of the USA. East coast versus the adventurous and Asian-influenced perspective of the West coast), it is important that policies be created so that these viewpoints can "truly become blended instead of siloed off." Thus, by creating opportunities for exposure to new ideas and ensuring that diverse viewpoints are welcomed and respected, organizations can ensure that diversity translates into greater innovation.

It is also important that diverse workers take steps be their own advocates and ensure their ideas are not overlooked in favor of the status quo. Employees of all backgrounds should be encouraged to engage in the common discourse, express a willingness to learn, and speak up or even challenge the ideas of others they disagree with. To aid this, employees should be provided ample leisure time to recover their energy and pursue their own passions. By nurturing rich relationships with family and friends outside of work, people can be exposed to new ideas that can enrich their work. Even within the organization, it is critical to create an environment where people with diversified passions can find their outlet (e.g., affinity clubs and volunteer opportunities) to maintain peak levels of energy and motivation.

CONCLUSION

In this chapter, we have argued that innovative organizational cultures feature three important pillars: psychological safety, openness to new ideas, and the celebration of diversity. Though critical, we close by acknowledging that fostering such flexible and agile cultural norms becomes increasingly more difficult as companies expand globally and grow in size. This is because customers of global brands often expect a universal standard, making true customization and localization of products difficult to execute. This concern for adopting an adaptive and truly *glocal* approach was expressed most directly by Xiaolin Yuan, the President and CEO of the Asia Pacific Region for Volvo Cars. He believes that for multinational companies there must be a clear, crystalized culture that is exemplified by upper management, which can then be emulated throughout the company and its presences around the world. Despite the clear value of establishing an agile and empowering organizational environment, it is not easy to maintain such a culture, particularly as companies scale up over time and become dispersed around the globe. Illustrating this challenge, Mats from Scania shared that

> *one principle that we have always treasured to try and balance risk-taking with managing risks. Unfortunately, what we saw in the past was that it became more about managing risks than encouraging people to try new things. We now need to try and regain the balance.*

As organizations are still accountable to investors, there needs to be a careful tension kept between control or accountability on the one hand and freedom to experiment on the other. With time, employees become more similar, and the culture becomes more entrenched, meaning the top leaders must continuously audit whether they are leaning too much in one direction or the other. Mats from Scania also contended that multinational companies could learn from China's unique mode of innovation described in Chapter 3. Citing the fact that his 130-year-old company recently enjoyed its most successful six months ever, he credited finding a balance between the traditional innovation method of creating a perfect product and bringing it to market with the Chinese model of releasing a basic or unfinished prototype to the market and allowing consumer demands to drive iterative development. In sum, we contend that many companies can retain their historical and centralized cultural roots while still creating an environment where all employees engage in open communication and feel safe and supported enough to bring new ideas to the fore.

The next three chapters will explore the conditions for achieving a truly innovative culture. There are three elements that must work in conjunction to become innovative to the core. It is important to note that these are not only the components of culture, but culture also feeds into these three facets in a reciprocal manner. These three factors emerged from our survey on innovation. In the Fall of 2020, we received 950 responses from executives (over 38% were CEO, GMs, or Owners) from a variety of functions (58% in the head office, 12% marketing, 8% project management, 7% finance, and 15% other functions) and industries (25% manufacturing, 16% services, 16% tech, 8% healthcare, 8% finances, and 27% other). These three facets emerged as the critical components of innovative cultures: leadership behaviors, talented employees, and organizational norms and systems (Fig. 5.1).

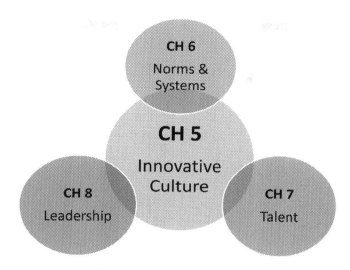

Fig. 5.1. Innovative Culture Components

ACTION POINTS

Create an Organizational Culture that Values Innovation

Innovation comes from a culture that allows agility and freedom in both policies and in communication among employees. Such cultures empower employees to follow their passions in alignment with the company strategic objectives.

Promote Psychological Safety

Innovative organizations create environments in which people feel free to go against the group's or leader's opinion. Employees are free from the fear of making intelligent mistakes that are aligned with clear business priorities.

Foster Openness

Open communication fuels creativity because employees benefit from peer and boss feedback and are exposed to new ways of thinking. A way to foster this, organizations should create a physical office design that promotes communication and establish rules for periods of individual work without interruptions. Leaders should work to eliminate organizational silos, reduce hierarchy, and allow communication across hierarchical levels.

Hire for Diversity

Diversity is a key ingredient for innovation. Hire people from diverse professional backgrounds, including differentiated thinking styles, genders, and nationalities. Only in psychological safe environment will people feel comfortable sharing their diverse perspectives and opinions, and only in open environments will this exchange of ideas even occur.

NOTES

1. https://medium.com/@antoniomartina/7-lessons-from-innovation-and-entrepreneurship-by-peter-f-drucker-d7953127b3b5

2. http://panmore.com/apple-inc-organizational-culture-features-implications#:~:text=Apple%20Inc.%20has%20an%20organizational%20culture%20for%20creative,and%20a%20mindset%20that%20challenges%20conventions%20and%20standards

3. https://www.apple.com/careers/sg/shared-values.html

4. https://hbswk.hbs.edu/item/make-your-employees-psychologically-safe

5. https://hbr.org/2021/01/your-best-ideas-are-often-your-last-ideas

6. https://hbr.org/2019/12/why-move-fast-and-break-things-doesnt-work-anymore

7. https://medium.com/@sathishvista/how-do-not-disturb-day-can-improve-your-productivity-5d5c43c85bf5

8. https://journals.sagepub.com/doi/abs/10.1016/s0149-2063_03_00033-3

9. https://onlinelibrary.wiley.com/doi/full/10.1002/jocb.443

6

AGILE ORGANIZATIONAL NORMS AND SYSTEMS

If you set up a system that forces employees to comply with certain things that they are not happy with, they're not going to be working for your company long. If you just hire a whole bunch of people, even though they might be geniuses, and put them individually in a cubicle, you're not going to have a great culture. Culture comes from the interaction among people and is the glue that holds people together.

— Kern Peng, Lab Head at Intel

INTRODUCTION

Although the values that make up the organizational culture are critical for innovation, these abstract concepts must be operationalized with the right norms, systems, and practices. Agility is perhaps the most critical feature of organizational norms and systems that foster innovation. The concept of agility originated in the IT world. The idea is to use an interactive process of development, with trials and corrections, instead of the traditional water fall development with specific steps and launch of the final product. This model was then applied by organizations as the Swedish company Spotify in the music digital distribution and even in the finance industry as the Dutch bank ING. An agile organization respond quickly to changes in their environment. To achieve this agility, managers and employees prioritize psychological safety, openness, and diversity. Kern Peng, a Lab Head at Intel in the USA, eloquently explained the importance of having well-designed norms and systems to reinforce cultural priorities:

> *Every organization has a vision, which is something that you would like to achieve. From that vision, you will have a mission or a purpose statement. It's like a north star in the in the sky, guiding you. Once you define the mission, then you need to define what kind of people you need to do the things that are in vision and the mission that you put forward. When you identify the right people, you start looking into how you can get them. That will translate into the change that you need to make in your management system, your corporate systems, and also the culture. You want to start with your system first because your culture is built upon your system.*

To encourage innovation, it is important to eliminate unnecessary layers of bureaucracy that can hinder open communication and quick decision-making. In addition to this, the right systems and norms will attract and retain the talent that you need to generate innovation.

In this chapter, we outline some of the best practices we uncovered from our interviewees in terms of norms and systems that boost innovation. Together, these practices create an agile organization that is flexible enough to implement new innovations and responsive to changing technologies and consumer demands.

INNOVATION STORIES

Communication Without Barriers at 3M by Kenneth Yu

There was a big earthquake in Sichuan Province in China and many people died. In China when something like that happens, the entire country wants to help. After an earthquake, one of the big problems is drinking water. People can donate tents, they can donate food, they can donate instant noodles, but people also need fresh water. Initially, people sent bottled water. Imagine the number of empty bottles, the trash it created. 3M has a method of filtering untreated water to become potable. There was young marketing assistant that had been with the company only a few months. She had the idea of donating 3M filtration systems. There was enough food and enough tents but water was still a problem. She thought it would be nice if 3M could donate 1,000 filtration systems, which would cost roughly 200,000 USD in total including installation.

She mentioned it to her boss and her supervisor told her to talk to me, the president, directly as I was the only person that could authorize this quickly. My secretary came to me and told me that this young employee has an idea, and she would like to talk to me. "Of course," I said, "tell her to come in." She presented the story, and then she said that she needs the authorization for these filters. I did not even ask how much it would cost. I told her to inform her boss and go ahead with the donation. That's our culture. This is just the atmosphere that people can talk to different levels when there is a need. We are not worried about rank. That's our culture. Quite frankly, I feel very proud of our culture.

In the rest of the chapter, we will explore different initiatives at organizational level that can make an organization more agile.

BREAK ORGANIZATIONAL SILOS

Agility must be embedded in the organizational structure. One of the principal ways that top management can enable agility is to create corporate structures that enable quick decision-making and facilitate communication across the ranks. As an example of this, Xiaolin Yuan, the President and CEO of Asia Pacific for Volvo Cars, described how his firm restructured their sales and marketing teams. Although previously these functions all reported to a single Senior Vice President, they later divided these reporting lines into three geographical regions. This structural change built in more flexibility and agility in decision-making, particularly for the Asia Pacific region, which is extremely dynamic and prone to constant change. Xiaolin noted that:

> By adapting our business in this way, we empowered our regions on many different levels and made them more agile. The interdepartmental communication is now far more effective. They can now collaborate more freely and effectively with the industrial side of our business. They can meet on a weekly basis, giving them the ability to adapt, make decisions, and be lighter on their feet.

At the regional level, by grouping all the functions for a single region in one central location, the strategy, design, engineering, production, and marketing teams can all converse and work seamlessly together to meet the market's unique needs. Such a structure, Xiaolin contended, allows large multinational organizations to react agility and remain competitive in local markets.

Zhifeng Zhang, the Managing Director of Hotelbeds in Shanghai, noted that a flat organizational structure is critical for innovation in his company. This is due, in part, to the fact that their B2B business model is unique for the industry, leaving little to no role models to imitate. By maintaining open lines of communication, he can quickly act on new ideas and make iterative adjustments according to real-time feedback from customers. Because Zhifeng reports directly to the global CCO, he is also able to feed successful ideas from the China market test field to the organization as a whole. Thus, the organizational structure allows changes and new innovations to be quickly developed and adopted. Prior to his appointment, there were many more layers of management, with the Chinese team reporting to 28 superiors in the global company. After the compression of the management chain, Zhifeng can much more easily pitch ideas to the board of directors, the global Investment Committee, and the global Innovation Committee for discussion.

Cameron Johnson, a Partner at Tidalwave Solutions, also believes that a flat organizational structure can enable the open communication norms that fuel innovation. He shared that in the most innovative organizations,

> *pushing against the status quo is normal, particularly in software or high technology industries. Questioning your boss in the open is common. Many organizations now are flat. In some companies, anyone can go to the CEO or the boss and just ask a question. You don't have to go through layers of management or processes to get an answer, particularly in the newer companies.*

To facilitate this dialogue, it is important that top managers don't hide in their corner offices, but rather proactively get involved with frontline processes and have conversations with the people who directly interact with customers or build your products. Organizations should also reward employees who come up with disruptive innovations. As good examples of this, Cameron pointed to companies like Google and 3M that allow employees a certain allocation of their time to work on new pet projects and shares any profits that come from these innovations with the employees themselves. Often these passion projects emanate from the customers themselves. As Kenneth from 3M shared with us, "one of the clichés we use quite a bit is, 'if you've got a problem and don't have an answer, go ask the customer.'"

INNOVATION STORIES

Discovery's Flat Organizational Structure by David Ferreira

I come from Discovery, a South African company in the
financial services industry, including health insurance.
I think it is impossible to imagine a corporate environment
that is flatter than the one prevailing at Discovery. One of
my most memorable experiences was when I first arrived at
the firm as a relatively senior hire from the outside. I was
fortunate enough to travel to all of Discovery's offices, and
meet the leaders of all the businesses all over the world. I
interviewed them, and spent time with them. One of the
first people that I interviewed was a very senior person in
South Africa, a wonderful man who is currently the CEO
of Discovery Bank. At the end of my introductory meeting
with him, I said:

> Listen, for somebody who's coming into a new envi-
> ronment and new culture, I try to do the right thing
> so that I don't create discord and noise. I want to
> bring my value, but I want to do it in a way that is
> helpful, not discordant. Can you tell me the answer
> to these two questions: If I want to contribute con-
> structively within the culture of Discovery, what
> is one thing that I should do, and one thing that I
> shouldn't do

He thought for a minute, and he said:

> One thing you should do is always give your hon-
> est opinion. Whoever you are meeting with, you
> should say what's on your mind, and you should
> contribute your thoughts. if you do that in a way
> that is respectful and not personal, and is well-
> intentioned, you should feel free to say whatever
> you like in whatever forum. That's what we're look-
> ing for from you.

I said: "OK, that's fantastic; it's great to hear. Now what's the one thing that I shouldn't do?" He thought for a while, looked up at the ceiling, and said: "There's nothing you shouldn't do." That, to me, is the epitome of a flat organization. The genuine ability to speak your mind directly to the company's senior leadership in a way that is unconstrained.

BE RESPONSIVE AND MAKE RAPID DECISIONS

Many of our interviewees highlighted that the Chinese business landscape offers several lessons on how leaders can be more agile and responsive in today's volatile, uncertain, complex, and ambiguous (VUCA) world. Jari Grosse-Ruyken, a Managing Partner of the consulting firm, hivetime, suggested that the linear and structured method of new product development championed by many German and other Western organizations is simply too slow be able to capitalize on constantly changing trends and consumer preferences. Instead, he opined, organizations should shift "to do less overthinking, to go more into rapid prototyping and trying things and seeing if they work." Others noted that certain organizational systems and processes can be implemented to support organizational agility.

Changjun Sun, a consultant at TÜV Rheinland, recalled that his organization was able to speed up the approval process for certifying suppliers by changing the location of the expert evaluation committee from Germany to China. Although German experts are still part of the committee, having the group located in China dramatically accelerated the approval process to a maximum of two months, which allowed for quicker decision-making. This experience led Changjun to conclude that "decisions must be made close to the market. It simply won't do if the decision makers are all 10,000 km away from the market. In this way, we have developed the current decision-making system. This system is very important as it can reduce the impact of individual factors as much as possible." Quick decision-making is particularly important when operating as a multinational in the China market because Chinese private companies have traditionally been able to make decisions faster than those who must get approval from an international headquarters. Zhenping Zheng, a Supervisor at Openex Intelligent Technology, agreed that having the right systems in place can help to remove barriers to innovation. In his organization, this takes the form of high levels of empowerment in each of the different functions. For example, the marketing department makes all the decisions about marketing without any intervention from top management.

Our research revealed that there are also several ways that top management can reinforce the effects of innovative systems and Norms through their own behavior. Cameron Johnson, a Partner at Tidalwave Solutions, suggested that the challenges brought by the COVID-19 pandemic in 2019 have served to underscore the importance of being flexible and adaptable as an organization. To create this agility, he suggests that leaders follow the example of Chamath Palihapitiya, a former Facebook executive, who makes a point of getting "on the front line, working with people, delving into information, and challenging assumptions." By creating an environment where people feel safe enough to challenge the status quo and by having top management actively communicate with employees to seek out new ways of doing work, large companies can stay nimble and responsive to change. Congwei Huang, the founder of Z-trip, agreed that the key to constant innovation is to maintain close tabs on customers. He believes that this is critical

> *because users know you and what they want the best. We require our customer managers to ask customers seven questions, among which, three questions are about asking users what we can improve.*

This process of keeping open lines of communications with customers has been institutionalized within Z-trip, with the customer success team being required to visit a minimum of 10

customers per month and bring back the answers to the prescribed questions. From there, the product managers will explore
opportunities to develop products that can resolve the pain points
raised by customers.

Some organizations take customer-driven innovation to the
extreme. For example, David Wang, the President of Buhler China
and Asia Pacific, noted that his company has more than 10 innovation laboratories around the world that work closely with customers to make changes depending on their feedback. He shared that
they serve various industries and customers in food and e-mobili-
ties, such as

> *a flour mill lab, a rice mill factory lab, a pasta lab, a choco-
> late lab, a coffee laboratory, a battery lab, and an optics
> technology lab. We have all kinds of applications and
> technology solutions. Why we do that? Because through
> these labs we can work more deeper with our customers,
> not only we provide a testing capability, but also provide a
> co-innovation capability together with customers.*

Buy encouraging customers to give feedback on new products
and services, they can learn more about the challenges they face
and their preferences so that the company can serve them better.
Jun Wang, the country president of Oerlikon China, agreed that
customer-assisted research and development is key for capturing a pioneering position in one's industry. To do this, his company keeps a close eye on ever-changing market demands and
also competitor behaviors. It is only by coming up with consistently creative responses to changing demands that companies
can stay profitable. Jun succinctly summarizes this philosophy
by concluding that "without innovation, there is no future. You
can never stay in your comfort zone and expect to profit off
it forever."

There are also several ways that top managers can reinforce the
adoption and expression of cultural norms that foster innovation.
One is to ensure that there is a large and dedicated team devoted
solely to research and development (R&D). As an example of this,
an executive of the electric vehicle company, NIO, states that they

employ over 2,000 people on the R&D team. They also have innovation listed as a key priority of the company's five-year strategy. To maintain energy and passion in the company, they have instilled joy, friendliness, and high-quality service as their cultural pillars. The executive from NIO who wished to remain anonymous shared that their brand image has two core components:

> *The first is innovation, and the second is that the entire brand image of NIO is a bit cute, isn't it? Our logo is round. We are friendly to our customers. Thus, we focus on these two things: our customers and innovation. This environment encourages all of the employees to think like entrepreneurs and to strive to build a great company.*

INNOVATION STORIES

Technology-driven Sales Model Innovation at Kimberly-Clark by Jason Jin

We have introduced several sales model innovations at Kimberly-Clark by keeping up with several trends. The first one is e-commerce. We were the first diaper brand on the platform JD.com. Today our partnership with JD.com is still strategic. The next innovation was shifting to an online-to-offline (O2O) model. At the beginning of 2019, I realized that everyone had started to talk about O2O. So, we invited the CEO of one of the leading O2O platforms to teach our top leaders. We told the CEO that we didn't know much about this business. I still remember what he said in 2019:

> *Don't think that O2O is just about convenience. Whoever makes a call at the last minute and places an order online can receive their goods in an hour. That is a convenience store. If you think so, you are completely wrong. It's not the convenience that you talk about, it's the one-hour e-commerce. If it's one-hour e-commerce, you don't have to worry about whether you can sell your products*

> *on this platform. Diapers are stockpiled, but sani-*
> *tary pads are more likely to be sold at the last*
> *minute.*
>
> In O2O, we use our online channel to bring people to the
> physical store where they make their purchases. We real-
> ized that this is a new channel at the beginning of 2019,
> and immediately set up a team to focus on this channel,
> because we saw it as the future of e-commerce. At that time,
> our regular offline channels and other trade channels were
> shrinking. Turning to O2O was a bid to save them. We
> built our own capabilities in 2019 and offline sales depend-
> ed on this thing to maintain, otherwise offline would be
> a mess.

USE YOUR COMPETITION AS AN INNOVATION IMPETUS

Another factor that was highlighted by our interviewees was the
role of competition in fueling innovation. Jason Yin, the Chief
Financial Officer at Kimberly-Clark in China, described how technological advancements allowed local competitors to enter their
industry, forcing them to innovate in order to survive. He noted
that previously, their industry was protected by capital barriers giv-
en that each piece of manufacturing equipment costed more than
$10 million dollars each. In 2017, however, the production process
was dramatically simplified, and many local brands began to enter
the market in huge numbers. Because these new companies typically had lower personnel costs, they were able to compete even with
less efficient processes. Competition was then further increased by
the rise of e-commerce. Small local brands now had access to new
retail chains and were able to sell their products directly to customers without dealing with the traditional retail channels like Carre-
four and Walmart. Jason noted:

> *The threshold for e-commerce is not so high. You just need*
> *to make your product popular among internet celebrities,*

and then it will sell well. Many new local consumer brands rose up in this way. The other channel is offline small shops. Once the logistics are established, the shopkeepers realize that they don't need to buy and sell big-name products. They can find an OEM and stick a brand name onto their products, which are as good as the products of big brands. Then they can earn all the margins. This leads to the emergence of thousands of brands all at once, because every small shop owner can do this, and they feed the production lines in the supply chain.

CONNECT INNOVATION TO KEY PERFORMANCE INDICATORS AND REWARDS

One important component of an organizational system that drives innovation is to ensure that rewards are provided when managers and employees enact innovative behaviors and engage in the cultural norms defined in the previous chapter. Zhenping from Openex noted that in his company this takes the form of providing equity incentives to employees. By splitting 40% of the shares among employees, Openex signals that they are willing to share the profits and employees feel as though they can directly benefit when they contribute to the growth and success of their company. Jason from Kimberly-Clark agreed that rewards can be key drivers of innovative behavior. He added that it is important that incentives be as simple and straightforward as possible to avoid confusing employees with mixed priorities. As an example, he shared that in China's dynamic market, profitable growth is key. Hence, incentives are aligned with this performance criteria, but he has considerable latitude in determining how to achieve this growth. The electric vehicle company, NIO, also believes in nearly all employees holding company stocks so that they are directly invested in the growth and success of the organization as a whole over the long-term.

Over time, innovation processes must be balanced with efficiency and bottom-line concerns. Mats Harborn, the President of Scania China, suggested that organizations should strive to be both efficient and high-quality, particularly in China. He shared that "we need to combine China speed with the Swedish quality, and this is the big challenge." To do so, he suggests that multinational parent companies should give their China's branches more autonomy so that they can react to the unique speed and opportunities in this market. Another means of achieving this balance is to ensure that innovation is included in the key performance indicators (KPIs) of employees. Jerry Liu, the President of Cargill China, shared that his organization recently made a shift from purely focusing on earnings and returns on capital to including growth and innovation indicators in their performance measurement. David Wang, the President of Buhler China and Asia Pacific, also suggested that organizations should create a culture wherein employees do not focus single-mindedly on operational KPIs, but rather are encouraged to be more experimental and innovative. In this way, employees can balance innovation and efficiency. David further suggested that:

> First, the target must be realistic, and has to be a little bit of stretch. The second thing is to create an innovation culture and environment, empower the team, and then assist them. You empower them, but you also support them through it. They can have their own way of working through the process and achieving the target. They can try some experimental ideas which could achieve the KPIs or fail. I never punish failed experiments because you need to allow failure to happen for people to pioneer and try new things in their work. If their intention is good, and they want to do things better, I encourage that. I do not criticize people if they fail.

MAKE INNOVATION A CORE ORGANIZATIONAL VALUE

Strong organizational values can help managers avoid focusing too stringently on profits and efficiency at the expense of innovation. In addition to bottom-line indicators, a good practice is to rate have managers rate employees in terms of how well they enact the core values of the organization. Zhifeng Zhang, the Managing Director of Hotelbeds in Shanghai, shared that in his organization innovation indicators such as the growth in new customers and new product launches are included in the business KPIs for managers. Zhifeng believes that pairing a decentralized power structure with objective indicators that ensure that people are being held accountable for outcomes.

Though rewarding the right types of behaviors is critical, some respondents contended that incentives alone are not enough to motivate innovative behaviors. Congwei Huang, the Founder of Z-trip, shared that:

> I don't think rewards really drive creativity. I think the most innovative ideas come from people who have outstanding user perceptions. They are eager to create value, and they have their own dreams. These dreams cannot be reached by money or other incentives alone.

As a result of this passion for helping create a better user experience, he frequently sees people working 14-hour days in the innovation center. This does not come from management pressure, but rather an innate desire to please the client and make a difference in the lives of other. To ensure that innovations are useful and not just for the sake of making up something new, however, the company did formalize clear objective dimensions that are used to qualify a given innovation project. Thus, there is a transparent and quantifiable yardstick (rather than subjective management opinion) that is used to evaluate and reward innovative ideas.

QUICKLY APPROVE AND MONITOR INNOVATION PROJECTS

Many of the executives we spoke with shared their organizations' approval processes and norms for funding and monitoring new innovations. Shawn Hang, the founder of the Chinese sports platform, HUPU, provides a great example of this. Although people can come to him with ideas at any time, he also formally invites an external VC investment manager to review the innovative projects in the company. He asks the external team to determine whether they would invest in the employees' ideas and, if so, how much they would pledge. Based on this information, he chooses which projects and ideas to support financially within the mother organization. He shared that

> *with this system the team will have a different perspective. They see themselves not as trying to get approval from upper management, but from the capital market. It's the best test.*

Changjun from TÜV Rheinland has also instituted Norms with his team to ensure that the organization remains agile and open to new ideas. As an example, he shared that he has trained all the marketing people to never say no when a client asks them for something new or unheard of. Instead, they must bring the request to top management so that they can judge how feasible it would be to comply with the request. He believes this process has proven to be quite successful, with "some random orders, though small initially, turning big if you're the only one in the market providing this good or service, and the business will continue and grow." Another way that he proactively seeks innovation is by having a specialized team of people dedicated to searching the Internet for information about changes in the industry and evolving social needs. They then present this cultivated information to the heads of the sales and operations department twice a year to brainstorm how the company might be able to respond to emerging trends and opportunities. The team votes to determine the most promising ideas, and the top five projects are given a priority in technology, training, resources, and customer research. In this way, they are able to stay ahead of changes in the industry and provide new products and services well ahead of their competitors.

LEARN FROM FAILURE AND CREATE TRUST

Other companies emphasize the importance of making decisions as objectively and data driven as possible. For example, one technology product manager we spoke to stated that all new products at their company are subject to an impartial review. They shared that

> *this process is purely scientific, personal ideas and emotions are not to be involved. After this process, we try to determine whether there is room for improvement, or if it is simply a dead end.*

This objectivity also extends to how they manage their teams. Although they have a zero-tolerance policy for integrity violations, employees are not penalized for making mistakes in the pursuit of creativity. Experts agreed, however, that there should be limits when it comes to norms for tolerating mistakes in order to limit waste and inefficiencies. Jun Wang, the country president of Oerlikon China, has a policy that all people are "free to act" within the parameters of strict budgets. Each year, roughly 4–6% of their revenue is earmarked for research and development projects. Within these projects, employees have a large degree of behavioral latitude but must apply for special approval if they believe they will exceed their budgets.

There are also several things that managers can do to monitor the exact causes of failure to ensure that the organization learns from these events. Another Chinese General Manager we spoke with suggested that managers should investigate five aspects after employees fail. First, one should evaluate whether the innovation efforts have the potential to lead to increased profits. Following failure, managers should question whether the employee skills and resources devoted to the project were sufficient. Third, constant communication is needed to ensure that all stakeholders understand their goal and what portion of the whole they are accountable for. Fourth, managers should evaluate whether the innovation is simply ahead of its time. Finally, managers should determine whether the failure was accidental or inevitable because of a doomed start. Importantly, they contended that the leader should take responsibility for failures rather than letting employees take the blame. Doing so will increase trust and reduce fear of making mistakes. As they noted:

The reason why I keep interacting with employees all the time in public, workplaces, and private situations is that I think trust is important for innovation. As innovations can sometimes fail, at that time, the person in charge should be able to take the responsibility. If not, you will create negative feelings among employees at all levels. If they don't trust you, innovation cannot be achieved.

Once this trust is established, they suggested that managers should monitor the overall progress of project teams without concerning themselves with the details. As an example, only keeping track of profit margins for the team can empower them to find their best working style and enable them to act on creative ideas.

MAKE YOUR PROCESSES MORE AGILE

One differentiating factor of many of the world's most innovative organizations is to anchor their innovations and business processes on problem-solving rather than implementing new technologies. Mats claims that his organization, Scania, uses this systemic and problem-oriented approach for innovation. Like IKEA, they employ a modular approach wherein they use the smallest number of components possible and can put these components together in different ways to create many customizable variations. This modular structure allows the company to act on even small ideas, because often these involve adjustments to only a single component rather than a completely new design for an entire truck. A modular structure also enables innovation in service given that they can alter the design to accommodate client needs for timing and cost. He shared the following example of how innovation occurs in such a modular system:

When our engineers are working on the fuel efficiency of the combustion engine, they focus on one combustion chamber, one cylinder, because all our engines, no matter if it's a 5-cylinder, 6-cylinder straight design, or an 8-cylinder V8 design, they all have the same cylinder. We put

all the focus in one combustion chamber. Once that's opti-
mized, then we have optimized combustion for the whole
engine range.

FORM PARTNERSHIPS FOR INNOVATION

Another practice that organizations may use to drive innovation is
to invest in or acquire private companies that have created a new
technology, product, or service. As opposed to developing innovative solutions in-house, companies can choose to take over an existing company that is already excelling in the area that the central
firm wants to expand into. This strategy comes with its own challenges, however. Namely, it takes time to seamlessly integrate the
different cultures and norms of the organizations and the acquired
company can become frustrated by the newfound rigidity of the
parent company.

Jerry Liu, the President of Cargill China, noted that taking on
strategic partnerships can be another way that companies can
innovate. This is a somewhat newer form of innovation in his company. He recalled that:

> *For quite some time at Cargill, if we wanted to do some-*
> *thing, we did it ourselves. But we have realized that we*
> *cannot do everything ourselves. Today, we are more open*
> *to partnering with large companies like Starbucks, and*
> *with our suppliers. We also are trying to take a venture*
> *approach. Cargill is setting up a fund of around 100 mil-*
> *lion, with around 30 or 40 million earmarked for each*
> *venture. We let the venture to grow freely in the beginning*
> *before we take it over and run it.*

This form of outsourced and shared innovation allows the company to maintain its current level of efficiency while slowly introducing an entrepreneurial spirit into the larger organization. This
way, they can devote innovation resources into smaller organizations that are naturally more flexible.

CONCLUSION

Organizations that feature deep innovation often have organizational structures that are extremely flat and reporting lines that enable open communication. These structures ideally will be paired with strategically aligned rewards and KPIs that allow creativity to bloom. In doing so, organizational structures that are innovative to the core will allow for bottom-up innovation, create a modular work approach, and co-create innovation through acquisitions or partnerships. Within these innovative structures, managers can opt to allow employees ample funds and sufficient time to work on their passion projects. As noted in previous chapters, the world can also learn from China's unique model of rapid prototyping and incremental improvement to agilely adapt to changing external conditions.

ACTION POINTS

To Create an Agile Organization

Break Organizational Silos
Create corporate structures that enable quick decision-making and easy communication across the ranks. Group corporate functions close to the business region. Reduce levels in the organizational structure. Top managers should show proactivity and communicate with the frontline employees.

Be Responsive and Make Rapid Decisions
Reduce overthinking and use rapid prototyping to test new ideas. Accelerate the decision-making process without losing control. Create an environment in which employees at all levels feel free to challenge the status quo. Keep open lines of communication with your customers.

Use Your Competitors as an Innovation Impetus
Follow new local competitors. Do not ignore them because they are small. One day they can take your business over.

Connect Innovation to Rewards and KPIs

Rewards should promote innovative behaviors. Few rewards better than many as too many rewards might confuse employees with mixed priorities. Include innovation in your KPIs.

Make Innovation a Core Organizational Value

Including innovation as a core value can help organizations avoid a stringent focus on efficiency. The best ideas come from employees that have innovation as their own personal value.

Quickly Approving and Monitoring Innovation Project

Streamline the approval process. Invite external investors to evaluate new ideas. Train your marketing people not to say no to clients when they bring some new requests. Ask them to bring ideas to top management. Create a specialized team to search the internet for new ideas and business models.

Learn from Failure and Create Trust

Create ways to limit mistakes to control waste and unnecessary risks. Leaders to create trust should take responsibility for failures rather than blaming employees.

Make Processes More Agile

Anchor innovation on problem-solving rather than on just implementing new technologies.

Form Partnerships for Innovation

Invest or acquire private companies that have created a new technology, product, or service. This will allow the company to introduce an entrepreneurial spirit to the organization.

7

ATTRACTING AND CULTIVATING INNOVATIVE TALENT

The bottom line is that innovations come from people. So, the people in your organization should be your main focus if you want innovation.

– Kern Peng, Lab Head at Intel

INTRODUCTION

Although proper leadership and setting the right organizational climate are essential, another piece of the innovation puzzle is ensuring that the organization can recruit and retain the right talent to drive innovation in the organization. Kern Peng, a Lab Head at Intel, summarizes this idea succinctly by stating that "with people, the key ingredients for any individual to do innovation are *capability* and the *willingness* to do things." Thus, having workers that are both highly competent and highly motivated is essential to fueling innovation. Some interviewees suggested that it is more important to ensure that the workforce engages in certain behaviors rather than possesses any specific characteristics. As Kamal Dhuper, the CEO of NIIT China, noted,

> *every organization needs talent that is willing to adapt, change, and is prepared for the future of work. It could be the same talent that every other organization has, but the sensitivity and the understanding that you need to learn and develop new skills to be able to succeed in the future of work are essential.*

In addition, it is important that organizations get all departments aligned under the goal of innovation and ensure that the right behaviors and achievements are rewarded. Changjun Sun, a consultant at TÜV Rheinland in China, underscored this final point, noting that

> *despite the company's emphasis on innovation, if the employees cannot see benefits of doing so, or if they see any benefits as accidental rather than deliberate, the incentive mechanism for innovation will be weakened.*

Several recent reports have underscored the importance of access to prime talent pools for innovation. Further supporting our conclusion in Chapter 2 about the readiness of certain countries for innovation, the IMD World Talent Ranking 2020[1] suggests that certain countries are comparatively better at investing in, developing, and attracting high-skilled workers. Countries that invest in every stage of the education process, are open to diverse people and ideas, and make their countries pleasant and affordable places to live cultivate the most talented workforce. In their latest ranking, many of the top 25 countries are the same ones that have been profiled throughout this book. These include Switzerland (#1), Sweden (#5), Singapore (#9), the USA (#15), Israel (#22), and the UAE (#24). Likewise, INSEAD's 2021 Global Talent Competitive Index[2] reveals that the COVID-19 pandemic uncovered strengths and weaknesses in how different countries developed and retained talent. Many of the high-income economies that invested heavily in both education and employee support remained competitive as workers rethought their careers, locations, and preferred modes of work. Because of this, we find many familiar names at the top of INSEAD's ranking, including Switzerland (#1), Singapore (#2), the USA (#3), Denmark (#4), Sweden (#5), Israel (#21), the UAE (#25), South Korea (#27), and China (#37).

In this chapter, we highlight several factors that emerged from our research related to how organizations can target, hire, and motivate a high-quality and innovative workforce. These include recruiting young and creative workers, cultivating a culture that makes diverse, high-quality recruits feel like they belong, and ensuring that people are supported with the resources they need to propel their careers forward and engage in entrepreneurial pursuits. We delve into each of these factors in more detail in the sections that follow.

INNOVATION STORIES

Young Employees at Kimberly-Clark Tap Unique Consumer Insights by Jason Yin

I remind myself every day that the experience that many managers are so proud can easily become a burden. Keeping pace with the times means that we need to truly understand our current consumers. Consumers today in China are very different from past generations. For example, in an effort

to name a new product, several senior leaders thought that
"Zhangzhongbao," which means "palm treasure" should be
used, but several young marketing managers rejected that
idea. They thought that this name only showcased the function, and they wanted to make the new name have more of
an emotional connection for consumers. They suggested that
we call it "Maozhua" or "Cat's Claw" instead. We thought
this would not work because it is not easy to pronounce in
Chinese. I recall the senior leaders, including myself, who are
over 50 years old, debating with the marketing folks who are
in their 20s.

They insisted on calling it "Zhuaxinbao" because the
name is cute and young people love cats. They asked us to
trust them, and finally, we gave in. To be honest, the reason why we compromised is that we thought it is a niche
market and has low risk, so we allowed them to have a try.
Looking back, that probably was a smart decision. Three
months after launching the product, we doubled sales
when compared to our main competitor's product sales
online. The advertisement immediately attracted praise
and the product gained popularity. This story shows us
that debating different perspectives is crucial and that the
leadership must be willing to accept new ideas, otherwise
we won't succeed.

IDENTIFY TALENT THAT FITS WITH THE CULTURE OF INNOVATION

Our interviewees shared several things they look for in prospective
employees as well as tips on how best to attract and onboard these
workers. Cheng Hang, the founder of Chinese Internet company
Hupu, judges applicants on three primary criteria: whether they
are team players, proactive, and intelligent. He elaborated further
on these factors as follows:

> First, they must be a good person. Some people are, I don't
> want to say evil, but they are selfish or self-centered. You

need to be a good person with a good heart. Secondly, you need to be intelligent. I think everybody who has four years of undergraduate education in China, or the US will fit my criteria. It's not that high. And third, he needs to be self-driven, very self-driven. These are my three criteria.

He believed that by hiring people who meet these three criteria and by giving them the tools and resources to pursue their own entrepreneurial passions, innovation can easily occur within the organization. Similarly, Congwei Huang from Z-trip focuses on testing candidates' basic intellectual abilities as well their moral bottom lines. Of the two, when he interviews candidates, he "pays more attention to their moralities. The moral criterion doesn't have an upper limit, but we set serious bottom lines. I think my bottom line of selecting employees is their moral standard." In contrast, Yang Bing, the founder of DEWU in China, focuses primarily on identifying competent and hard-working candidates, noting that "the people we recruit are all smart people who can do work. Our slogan is that smart people work hard together."

Many of our interviewees were adamant that innovation requires recruiting enough young employees. Congwei Huang, the Founder of Chinese tech company, Z-trip, noted that he likes to continuously hire a healthy percentage of fresh graduates to work the frontline because

young people know better what other young people need. We must keep the company up with the times to be innovative. Our requirements are to work for customers and absorb more young talents.

Similarly, Zhenping Zhen, a supervisor at Openex Intelligent Technology company, shared that he looks for people who are naturally curious and able to sense new opportunities. Given that curiosity is often most evident among students, they attach a great importance on maintaining close ties with the alumni and placement departments at prestigious schools including Xiamen University and Jiaotong University.

Despite the advantages of youth, others emphasized that poaching more seasoned – but currently unhappy – employees from other companies can also be a fruitful strategy for innovation. As an example, Zhenping from Openex seized the opportunity to acquire the entire R&D team from one of the world's largest companies that happened to be struggling at the time. By successfully hiring an in-tact team, he was able to begin producing high-quality equipment in a very short time span. He also saw the common practice of rival companies hiring younger employees to replace older ones as something that works to his advantage. To illustrate this point, he shared the story of another recent recruit:

> *Last year, I attracted a partner who had been in Huawei for many years. You know, in Huawei, employees are no longer needed once they turn a certain age. He was willing to join us because we are innovative, and we can give him the space to follow his own passions. Although his salary is roughly 50% of what he made at Huawei, we offered him 40% of his old salary in equity. He also has the full right to distribute the equity flexibly to his team. This means that he takes the lead of the team. He is excellent technically and his team is very stable and the members under him are highly influenced by him.*

By making this older worker feel respected and helping him grow his skillset through exposure to customers in the sales aspect of his job, the company was able to hire and motivate a high-quality and creative R&D leader despite being unable to offer the high salary of the large high-tech companies.

Kenneth Yu, the former President of 3M China, also shared that his company had a policy of hiring people with at least two years of working experience. He noted that often this means they have been conditioned to work in environments where they primarily execute the orders of others rather than trying to find novel solutions themselves. To acclimate them to the innovative culture of 3M, he relies on both training as well as the work of his supervisors to transmit the corporate values and reward the right kinds of behaviors.

The respective advantages of both younger and older employees highlight another factor brought up frequently by interviewees: the need for diverse backgrounds and perspectives among employees. Zhifeng Zhang from Hotelbeds in Shanghai deliberately looks for people who are passionate and have diverse points of view. He shared that

> *they should have their own initiatives and ideas. We do not look for a specific type of person, but I believe that this quality is very important, and I value it very much because we are still in the stage of entrepreneurship.*

Cameron Johnson, a Partner at Tidalwave Solutions, similarly opined that

> *the more diverse an environment is, the more input you get from each other, which further spurs innovation. And I think this is now a universal idea that if organizations want to encourage innovation, they need to create very diverse work environments.*

He cautioned against dismissing ideas that appear non-traditional or foreign out of hand, and instead believes that the most innovative organizations integrate diverse perspectives into the prevailing systems to come up with the best ideas. As another example of the power of diversity, Huijie Hong, the Founder of MITS Shanghai Technology, shared that:

> *Our recruits are versatile talents who are professionals in both technical skills and business communication. Thanks to the uniqueness of each factory, manager, equipment, and control system, each variation leads to a completely new series of events. That is why we need a human touch, to identify and to determine how to best customize the service. In the later processes such as negotiating with clients and implementing solutions, it is still essential to be constantly seeking new solutions to our clients' demands. Because of all these, we expect more than technical skillsets from a candidate, there should also be social and emotional qualities.*

Huijie of MITS also noted that although diverse perspectives are critical for fueling innovation, managing different cultures requires extra time and care. As an example, he shared that he had to make significant efforts to train his German and Singaporean partners in understanding the nuances of Chinese business culture. For example, he coached them on how to be less straightforward with Chinese clients, instead approaching them with an attitude of concern for their needs and cooperation. Similarly, Jun Wang, the country president of Oerlikon China, emphasized the special care that was taken to ensure that the German and other international specialists who joined his R&D center in China had a smooth transition and felt comfortable and welcome in their new home. These efforts were well-rewarded, as two of the original German specialists are still in China and have since developed highly innovative local teams and have gained connections and experiences that have propelled their own career trajectories.

As a potential alternate model of leveraging diverse talent, Roy Chason, the founder of KnoHao, suggested that companies in more homogenous cultures might benefit from bringing in a subset of foreign professionals and overseas returnees into their organizations as part of a specialized unit. By creating small pockets of innovation, these foreign perspectives can be intermingled, and these employees can be encouraged to take calculated risks that are separate from the operations of the primary organization. He cited Alibaba as an example of a company that recruits hungry young Chinese entrepreneurs with global experience as well as foreign talents and incubates their ideas in a group separate from the local coders.

COMPANY SNAPSHOT
Diversity as an Innovation Driver at Apple[3]

Apple's market value exceeded US$2 trillion for the first time on August 19, 2020, due in large part to its world-renowned commitment to cutting edge innovation. Its employees dedicate themselves to generating innovative ideas and transforming these into novel products at record speeds. To abate consumers' insatiable hunger for novelty,

Apple encourages innovative thinking. As an example of how they create this ecosystem, John Ternus, Vice President of Engineering, once said

> *whenever we want to build a new product, our team can use any angle during the development process to expand the imagination; the purpose is to make the product better. They are not limited by the rules and regulations of the established plan. I will not prescribe when a certain process must be completed for myself, nor will I bind myself to the development concepts of some old products.*

Apple is quite good at seeking innovative inspiration and has a habit of constantly improving products based on both the needs of the customers as well as the supply chain. In the end, though, a customer-focus is key. "Apple obsesses over the user experience, not revenue maximization," says one former Apple executive. In practice, this means that even when the short-term costs are higher, they persevere with the course of action, often leading to tremendous long-term financial rewards. Moreover, this customer-focus is not limited to a single geographical region. As an example, the creation of specific language keyboards, QR Code scanners, 5G, and night mode, were, in many ways, inspired by the needs of Chinese customers.

In addition, Apple sometimes asks suppliers to provide technologies and features that have never appeared on the market and that they have never tried to make before. Almost every new Apple product uses materials, formats, and technologies that are completely novel. Fueling these new ideas, Apple prides itself on fostering an innovative corporate climate. Tim Cook, the CEO, once shared that

> *what we do is we have a culture of creativity and a culture of collaboration. And these two things together, when they intersect, create enormous*

> *innovation. You put people together that have dif-*
> *ferent skills, that look at the world differently,*
> *maybe they're from different places, they have dif-*
> *ferent backgrounds. Some are hardware, some are*
> *software. Some are services. Some may be musicians*
> *and artists. But you put them all together on a com-*
> *mon purpose, to design an incredible product, and*
> *it is amazing what can come out of it.*

Finally, Apple doesn't limit itself to internal talent, but also cooperates with expertise outside the firm. For example, Apple has partnered with Stanford University to conduct its Apple Heart research, which is also the largest research effort of its kind. In sum, prioritizing diversity and meeting the needs of customers is what makes Apple successful.

CREATE INVITING ENVIRONMENTS TO ATTRACT DESIRABLE RECRUITS

Once organizations have identified what types of employees, they would like to hire to fuel innovation, leaders should ensure that they foster norms and office environments that will be attractive to these applicants (linking it to the other two parts of our innovation model). Doing so is critical because if employees do not feel supported and empowered in their new firms, they will likely grow frustrated and unmotivated, and will soon look elsewhere for employment.

INNOVATION STORIES

Office Design for Innovation[4]

Kern Peng from INTEL states that:

> *When a person walks into a company, their first impres-*
> *sion is based off the workplace's physical environment.*
> *There is not second chance for a first impression and*
> *that first impression is based on how people feel.*

Making a positive first impression is particularly important if companies want to attract and retain employees hoping to express their creativity and make their own mark. Although the physical environment of the office is not the only criteria, it can play an important role in employees' decisions to stay.

Despite this fact, many companies have offices that are dull and uninspiring. They design the office layout for efficiency, resulting in the ubiquity of so-called "cubicle farms." In contrast, innovative companies often feature open-plan layouts wherein people can communicate and collaborate easily, retreating to quieter sections of the office for individual work. Peng indicates that companies in Silicon Valley were among the first to decorate their offices with art and vivid colors, and that this "aesthetically pleasing environment not only attracts an artistic mindset, but also encourages employees to keep the creative spirit alive."

Peng also believes that the office environment should differ based on the type of job. Accounting and Finance functions need environments that are conducive to long hours of concentration with few interruptions. Jobs that require innovative ideas should be done in environments that allow for open communication and information sharing. Colors also matter. Cold colors like blue are better for concentration and reflection, whereas warm colors like orange create energy. Example of companies that experiment with the look and layout of their physical work environment include Google, Pixar, Swatch, Facebook, and ING, among others.

Peng concludes that companies need to create work environments that will make the type of employees they are hoping to hire feel comfortable and as if they belong. To this end, many innovative companies allow employees to personalize their space and even bring their pets to work. He adds that when an inspiring work environment is paired with work that is interesting and challenging, "people will devote themselves to achieving results that may often exceed your expectations."

In our 2020 CEIBS Innovation Survey Report, we highlight employee norms and behaviors as one of the three key components of an innovative culture. We found that employees will be most likely to unleash their innovation when they are unafraid to raise concerns or fail, are allowed to experiment, can openly communicate with others, and are highly competent and independently motivated to learn. When respondents worked in environments that contained this type of talent and support, they were far less likely to report that they wanted to leave the organization. Somewhat worrisome, however, is the fact that respondents to our CEIBS Innovation Survey believed that factors like providing employees candid feedback, hiring competent and curious employees, and allowing employees to safely express their opinions and concerns were the *least* important factors for fostering innovative climates. This reveals a disconnect between top management beliefs and the features that are likely to impact whether top talent stays or goes.

Our interviewees shared several fruitful ideas for how they attract and retain innovative talent in their own firms. Several executives described the importance of differentiating yourself from rival firms to attract people with the innovative spirit to drive innovation. For example, Cheng Hang from Hupu believes that offering resources for employees to pursue their own entrepreneurial ideas sets his company apart from many others in China. He observed:

> *In China nowadays, very few people actually want to help people to become an entrepreneur. For example, family members usually want a steady income. They don't want them to take risks. If you work in a company, your upper management doesn't want you to start your own business. In fact, they make you sign non-competition agreements to prevent this. They might even bring a lawsuit if you jump to a different company or start your own business. Entrepreneurs can be very lonely. Probably the only guys that are helping them or wishing them to success are angel investors and VCs. But in this industry, their selection criteria are so high. You must graduate from an Ivy League*

or work in Huawei or ByteDance for a few years. You basically have to be a genius to get funding.

By offering creative recruits the time and funds to pursue their own ideas while working within a stable organization, his organization creates a supportive and welcoming home for these innovative and entrepreneurial employees. Zhifeng Zhang at Hotelbeds in Shanghai also believes that the unique work norms of his organization help to attract top employees. In contrast with many top Chinese internet companies like Meituan, Ctrip, and Fliggy, his company offers employees a high level of work–life balance. He shared:

We do not have the '996' working system (work from 9 am to 9 pm 6 days per week). Foreign companies like us can't compete with [the local firms] when it comes to money, because we can't offer as many shares. We can only compete with them using our culture and our care for employees. Because our company is very flat, we have no brainwashing or bureaucracy. Leaders are not everything. We do not often work overtime. We do things in a simple way. Our architecture is very flat. On Saturday and Sunday, nobody will contact you and you do not have to read emails.

This unique culture helps to attract people who are not single-mindedly focused on money or meeting production objectives. Although they may lose some people who value this type of reward system, they attract creative people who want a healthy and balanced life with little to no hierarchy. Thus, the types of people who are likely to thrive in this innovative environment are those most attracted to work there. One idea may be to design two types of career tracks and compensation package: one for creative and innovative employees and another for more traditional functions such as accounting and finance.

For his part, Congwei Huang of Z-trip sees the brain drain of talent to the high-paying Internet giants to be at least partially positive. He uses careful exit interviews to first determine the cause of the attrition, sharing that:

> *People change jobs mainly for two reasons: they are either
> unhappy working in their original companies or the next
> company is more attractive. If they are unhappy work-
> ing in our company, we should find out the cause and if
> our company is less attractive than other companies, we
> should review whether it is because our company brings
> fewer benefits to our employees. At the same time, we
> also hope that talents who leave our company can create
> greater value outside. Maybe his show stage is not here,
> but in other places.*

This philosophy acts as a litmus test to ensure that they are con-
tinuing to foster the right culture and retain the people who fit best.
By assuring that employees are largely leaving for personal reasons,
they can also maintain good relationships and a positive reputation
in the industry.

Huijie Hong, the founder of MITS in Shanghai, also believes
that the treatment people receive from their supervisors will ultimately determine whether they will stay with the company and be
motivated to innovate. In his own firm, he tries to set an example
of this in his own daily behaviors. He shared:

> *I try my best to treat people with sincerity and integ-
> rity, that is why people are willing to work with me even
> though there are other opportunities …. In a word, trust is
> another keystone we built our business upon.*

Congwei Huang, the founder of Z-trip, also reiterated the importance of his team-building abilities and establishing competence-
based trust when asked about his company's success. By attracting
diverse team members (e.g., consultants and workers from different
industries) and making them feel welcome and valued, he was able
to uncover the company's competitive advantage. He shared that
initially they "held a lot of brainstorming meetings about entrepreneurship and also visited a lot of different customers and truly
listened to what they needed." Because the diverse team was able to
easily put themselves in the shoes of different types of customers,
they quickly concluded that there was a need for business travelers

to be reimbursed for canceled flights more quickly than the current timeline being offered by China's leading travel website at the time (e.g., cutting the time for some services from 20 days to 2 seconds). Thus, his ability to recruit diverse talent, bring them together under a unified vision, and value their input helped him to formulate a successful and highly innovative business model.

Zhenping Zheng from Openex also shared a recruitment strategy that is anchored on person-organization fit. He believes that "most employees that are resistant to openness and innovation and prefer to do clearly defined work, step-by-step." To create an attractive environment and emphasize that innovation is a priority, he encourages leaders to keep in touch with their own passions and to engage in storytelling with employees. "Instead of just giving them instructions, we need to tell them something that they can understand to mobilize their enthusiasm. It's very powerful to tell stories, specify needs, and clarify opportunities," he suggested.

Though this tool helps to underscore the mission and the meaningfulness of the work employees are doing, he acknowledged that it is also important to ensure that the compensation packages are competitive. Like other interviewees, he noted that he has lost many good employees to the Internet giants in recent years, simply because they are able to offer dramatically higher salaries. Jun Wang, the country president of Oerlikon China, also believes in the importance of competitive compensation and benefit packages, sharing that his firm views all employees are key stakeholders and offer packages that are in the 80th percentile in the industry. As a result,

> even [their] blue collar turnover is relatively low. For instance, staff turnover at [their] largest manufacturing plant, located in Suzhou industrial park, is only 10%, which is half of the park's average turnover rate.

Similarly, an executive at the Chinese carmaker, NIO, noted that their company offers shares to all newcomers after a six-month probation period in addition to high salaries. "Even when we were experiencing difficult times," they noted "we did not owe a penny to our employees." This helps to keep them competitive, and often they only lose employees to the biggest Internet giants of Meituan, Alibaba, and Toutiao.

Still, interviewees were adamant that financial rewards alone were not enough to motivate employee creativity and ensure retention. When paired with a baseline monetary recognition of the value employees bring, Jun Wang at Oerlikon China believes employees choose to stay because they are allowed decision-making latitude and are not punished for well-intended mistakes (though employees are held accountable for deliberately flouting company policies or regulations). With these norms in place, Jun believes that their "employees have sufficient resources to carry a team and assume responsibility along the way." Yang Bing, the founder of DEWU, believes that autonomy and flexibility can be key factors that attract innovative employees and allow them to do their best work. Although they ensure that there are common work hours so that employees can collaborate, the employees do have flexibility to work when they feel at their peak. In addition, employees are encouraged to work on passion projects so long that these are aligned with the company's overall mission. In this regard, Yang shared that "overall, we let colleagues do what they want to try, but we do not let them do things that have nothing to do with the company at this stage."

This flexibility has become perhaps even more of a desirable – or even demanded – feature following the COVID-19 pandemic, as many employees have realized firsthand the benefits of being able to flexibly accommodate their work and life demands.[5] This trend can also benefit company recruitment, however. With most employees now equipped with the skills to work remotely, firms can now select from a talent pool over a larger geographic region. Cameron Johnson of Tidalwave Solutions suggested that when organizations now need a specific skillset:

> *They don't have to look in the [Silicon] Valley anymore.*
> *With remote work, somebody in the Midwest can design*
> *their hardware or their software architecture or a marketer*
> *who lives in Minneapolis can be their unique marketer.*

Now, you not only don't have to rely on what's in your area, but now you have access to all kinds of different levels of talent, people, pay rates, and everything else that you couldn't have even a decade ago. With this trend, innovation not only will accelerate, but you will see people who historically would never have been involved in innovation driving change.

INNOVATION STORIES

Retaining Key Talent at Intel with Sabbaticals by Kern Peng

How does Intel keep retaining older employees? I've worked at Intel for 29 years, but in my department more than half the people have been working at Intel longer than I have. That shows you how stable the talent pool is at Intel. We talked about how systems impact culture and then culture impacts your capability to innovate. At Intel, our H.R. policies are obviously part of the system. We have a policy called sabbatical and this policy was implemented only a couple of years after Intel was founded. Every Intel employee after seven years can take eight weeks of time off with pay. If you add your vacation to this, you can take about three months off. If you have a new employee, and they leave after a couple of years, the impact is not that significant. You can just hire new employees to replace them. But if they leave after four or more years, and leave, that is a big loss for the company. With this 7th year sabbatical, the employee will think, why don't I just keep working until I earn this long time off, I can get refreshed or I can use that time to try out another job. If they want to change jobs, they can take three months off and start working at the new job. And if they are happy with the new job, they quit Intel. That's why people kind of keep holding on until that point.

There is another benefit of this policy. Before you take off for sabbatical, it's your responsibility to pass down whatever you do to the people that can cover you. It's up to you to work it out. If you're working on this project, you must train somebody else to take over. If this project is failing, when you come back to Intel, you will still be held accountable for it because you didn't pass down the knowledge correctly or didn't train them well enough to cover it. In most corporations, often the number one problem is that people typically gain skillsets, but they don't want to share because they feel like if they share everything they will be replaced. It's human nature to keep your skillsets to yourself to ensure job security. But at Intel, the sabbatical policy is that you must take this long time off or you will lose it, which is a big incentive to pass your knowledge to others.

The next issue comes when you come back to the company, you must face the fact that the company can function without you. When you come back, you may not get your old project back. You must find something new to do. I took three sabbaticals already. Every time I come back for the first couple of weeks, I don't know exactly what to do. I'm sitting in my office, and even though I'm a manager now, I passed my authority and responsibility to somebody else and the whole department can run without me. When sitting in my office, I realize that the company can operate without me and that my department can survive without me. By the way, the company won't pay me to sit around. I must do something. I must prove myself again. Time and time again, you can see the people that don't fit the Intel culture tend to leave on the first sabbatical. Some people leave because they don't feel like starting all over again. But do you know who stays after the first sabbatical? Those people that are not afraid of change, not afraid of training others, not afraid of giving out their skillsets, not afraid to teach others everything you know. That's an example of how a good system impacts the culture, talent development, and continuous innovation.

MOTIVATE THEM SO THEY STAY

After identifying the right types of employees and attracting them to your organization, there are several ways that deeply innovative organizations can ensure that veteran employees stay motivated and productive as the years pass. One important factor highlighted by our interviewees was helping employees to envisage their long-term career plans within the organization. In his role as a career advisor at Intel for the past 15 years, Kern Peng, a Lab Head at Intel, has advised people to consistently find the intersection of what he calls the TOP model. He elaborated that:

> *T stands for talent, O stands for opportunity, and P stands for Passion. These three circles connect at the center point, which represents the dream job for a given individual. If there is a job opportunity and you have the talent for it, but you don't have passion, it's just a job to make money. It's very difficult for you to go the long distance and do something that is wonderful and innovative. If you have the passion and talent but there is no job opportunity, it typically becomes a hobby rather than a career. In this model, we will prefer people to start with passion because passion is something you have total control over.*

Taking this model as a guide, Kern suggested that leaders should continuously check the passion levels of their employees and ensure that they both have the freedom to pursue their own ideas and are also exposed to new challenges and types of work to keep their motivation high over the long-term. He also advocated a systematic and step-by-step career planning system for employees based on their passions. Namely, employees can use their passions to help define their long-term goals (e.g., going from an engineer to the Chief Technology Officer). From there, you work backwards to determine what skill gaps remain to know which types of opportunities you should target in the interim. It is completely normal that these passions shift over time, requiring a corresponding shift in career goals. The important thing is that employees retain their motivation and are able to envision where they are going in their future with the company. In addition, the TOP model can also be scaled-up to talk about the overall culture of the company. Here, the passion component is reflected in the vision, mission, and values of the company. By communicating and embodying these, leaders can also create a meaningful and invigorating environment that keeps employees satisfied and productive. Of course, this passion must also be paired with strategic spotting of opportunities and keeping one's talent pipeline flowing and of high-quality.

There are also other innovative ways that organizations can retain employees by helping them to realize their own dreams. One example is helping to develop the skillsets they need to achieve their ultimate ambitions. Cheng Hang, the founder of Hupu and other ventures, created the Garden Lane School for his employees to learn how to become successful entrepreneurs. He shared that the students in this school are

> still managers or programmers in their companies, but they have the interest to start their own company sometime in the future. Garden Lane school provides an environment and certainly some resources to help them prepare to become an entrepreneur in the future.

Although it may seem ludicrous for many top managers to imagine giving their employees the resources to leave and start their own ventures, Cheng believes that this encouragement is the key to unlocking the potential of employees and keeping them motivated and creative during their time with him.

Finally, when developing employees and supporting their careers, it is important that the organization does not try to scale-up too quickly by bringing in all new talent. Instead, Xiaolin Yuan, the President and CEO of Volvo Cars for the Asia Pacific region, believes that sustainable growth is much better to ensure the growth and retention of people. Of course, growing this way takes much more time, but the end result is a more cohesive and versatile team that can drive the success of the company in the long-term. By establishing a reputation as an employer that grows leaders from within, you can also expect to recruit people who are attracted by this long-term prospect.

COMPANY SNAPSHOT

Volvo Cars

Upon its inception 1927, Gustaf Larson said: "Cars are made for people. The guiding principle behind everything we make at Volvo, therefore, is and must remain, safety." Volvo have always been pioneers in mobility; mobility that not just protects people, their loved ones and the environment, but also provides enjoyment and convenience. Their strategy is therefore to combine almost a century of delivering quality products with cutting edge investments into technology, to deliver a new experience built on fundamental values that mobility should be Personal, Sustainable, and Safe.

The brand has committed to developing and building the most personal solutions in mobility. In doing so, they aim to make life less complicated and to protect the freedom of their consumers to spend time and energy on the things that matter most. Simultaneously they also commit to the highest standard of sustainability in mobility and actively seek new ways of protecting the world by pioneering the safest and most intelligent technology solutions in mobility.

Volvo Cars announced the vision of full electrification in 2017, and in 2021 set ambitious objectives to have an all-electric range by 2030 and achieve carbon neutrality by 2040. The C40 Recharge marked the first Volvo model in history designed as purely electric. The brand continues to investment in their in-house battery and motor research and development and production with strategic partnerships to accelerate their electrification transformation.

The company's culture and their diverse workforce is central to their success. They regard attracting and retaining talent from all over the world as crucial, and endeavor to bring out the best in their people to deliver on their growth ambitions. By doing so, they remain a leading player in the highly competitive premium car and mobility industry.

On the 29th of November 2021 Volvo Cars welcomed over two hundred thousand new shareholders as they announced the outcome of the initial public offering and listing on Nasdaq Stockholm. The offering was substantially oversubscribed as it attracted strong interest from institutional investors in Sweden and abroad as well as from the general public in the Nordics. Volvo Cars has been trading on the Nasdaq Stockholm since October 29, 2021.

People trust the Volvo brand and know that it stands for something authentic and honest. But the language of next-gen mobility is changing. The brand recognizes the accelerating consumption sophistication among consumers, especially in China. To keep this relationship alive, Volvo extends its brand and product experience to consumers through a "multi-tentacled" consumer engagement and experiences, combining seamless offline to online experiences, innovative retail spaces, and the sophisticated minimalism unique to Volvo Cars.

Sources: https://www.volvogroup.com/en-en/about-us/history-and-r-d-milestones/r-d-milestones.html; https://group.volvocars.com/company;https://hj.pcauto.com.cn/wap/article/689087;https://news.58che.com/news/2145149.html

CONCLUSION

In this chapter, we highlight all the considerations leaders and organizations need to consider when selecting and retaining the right talent for innovation. These efforts are critical given that employees are the ones coming up with innovative ideas and putting in the work to make these ideas come to life. Our interviewees believe that the ideal employees for an organization that is innovative to the core should have diverse perspectives and should be youthful, energetic, experimental, and curious. To make environments that are welcoming to these types of employees, leaders should ensure that they cultivate attractive and vibrant workspaces while also reinforcing managerial norms that allow for ample autonomy and resources. By aligning employee passions and ambitions with the company's long-term goals, top leaders can create a family of employees with truly innovative mindsets.

ACTION POINTS

Identify Talent That Fits with the Culture of Innovation

Employees that are highly competent and motivated is essential to fueling innovation. Hire people that are team players, proactive, and intelligent. Recruit smart people that can work together. Look for people with diverse backgrounds and perspectives.

Create Inviting Environments to Attract Desirable Recruits

Differentiate yourself from rival firms. Foster norms and office environments that facilitate innovation. Allow employees to follow their own ideas that fit the company innovation strategy and provide resources to test those ideas. Welcome employees with entrepreneurial spirits. Creative people value work and life balance. Allow them to be in touch with their passions. Autonomy and flexibility attract creative people.

Motivate Them So They Stay

Help them to envisage their long-career plans within the organization. Establish career advisor role in your HR department. Expose them to new challenges and type of work. Create a meaningful company culture that resonates with them.

NOTES

1. https://www.imd.org/centers/world-competitiveness-center/rankings/world-talent-competitiveness/

2. https://www.insead.edu/sites/default/files/assets/dept/fr/gtci/GTCI-2021-Report.pdf

3. https://www.apple.com/watch/; https://m.huanqiu.
com/article/9CaKrnJR32L; https://www.bilibili.com/
read/cv9905944/; https://www.eco-business.com/opinion/
three-thoughts-on-apple-and-insanely-great-brand-leadership/

4. This mini case is based on an excerpt from Kern Peng's book *Project Management for Continuous Innovation*. (2018). Pike Publication, California.

5. https://www.cnbc.com/2021/09/20/a-hybrid-arrangement-might-not-be-what-workers-want-after-all.html

8

LEADING FOR INNOVATION: BEING A SERVANT AND AN ENTREPRENEUR

When you take a leadership role, when you have that position, people look at how you behave, what you talk about, what you reward, and what you try to discourage.

– Xiaolin Yuan, the President and CEO of Volvo Cars
Asia Pacific

INTRODUCTION

Leaders play an integral role in instilling a focus on innovation throughout every layer of an organization. Through their words, behaviors, and reward decisions they communicate the organization's priorities to their employees. Even if the top management counts innovation among its strategic goals and invests the money to redesign the physical spaces, organizations will likely make scant progress in this effort if leaders continue to micromanage employees, reward them only for efficiency, and punish well-intentioned mistakes. Leadership is so critical that David Ferreira, GM of Discovery Group in China, and also Deputy CEO of Ping An Health, views it as the most critical component of being innovative to the core. He believes that there needs to be an individual or a group that can convince people in the organization that change is needed, and adopt new methods of work that then trickle down through the organization. He concluded that "culture is obviously very important, but here's something that's even more important, which is leadership."

Kamal Dhuper, the CEO for NIIT China, shared some unique insights from the Adaptive Learning Organization Research Report released by his firm. This report counts a strong leadership culture as one of the key cornerstones of adaptive organizations. They define this as having leaders who are able to charismatically convince employees of why innovation and adapting to change are necessary. As tools in this mission, they recommend the use of storytelling both with sharing powerful visions from top management and when engaging in one-on-one conversations with people on the ground floor. While leaders are preoccupied with ensuring that everyone is motivated and aligned under unified goals, managers and lower-level employees should be empowered to make operations decisions to adjust to changing needs in the market. Leadership also emerged as one of three key indices of innovative organizations in our 2020 CEIBS Innovation Survey Report. Overall, smaller companies and those in the healthcare and services sectors tended to report that their leaders were committed to innovation, communicated innovative strategies to be a priority, and held managers accountable for driving innovation. Moreover, we found that 41% of respondents reported that new management techniques had been introduced in their organization in the last three years, which was considered the third most popular type of innovation that had been implemented. In this chapter, we will focus on the behaviors and messages shared by leaders that reinforce innovation and some of the leader characteristics that enable the behavioral norms and cultural pillars shared in previous chapters.

Our research revealed two primary characteristics of innovative leaders: they should be both a servant and an entrepreneur. We delve into each of these characteristics in more details below.

COMPANY SNAPSHOT

Discovery Group, South Africa

Discovery is a financial services group, listed in South Africa and with businesses around the world, that is founded on a "Shared Value" approach. Its current level of success has been achieved through a pioneering business model that incentivizes people to be healthier, allowing the insurance company also to benefit from the resulting lower risk profile of its customers. Started in the early 1990s, Discovery used a combination of medical science, data analytics, behavioral economics, and a new actuarial approach to innovate in the insurance industry, starting with health insurance. Discovery's co-founders, Adrian Gore and Barry Swartzberg, believed that the company's products needed not only to make money, but also have a positive impact on individuals and society. Using its Vitality wellness program as its strategic lynchpin, Discovery expanded into other insurance areas and financial services products and also entered new markets abroad. The flexibility of Vitality's structure allowed it to enter markets where it could never by itself become a leading insurer; where the barriers to entry were too high. Discovery instead chose to partner with established insurers in those markets by scaling the Vitality model as needed. In the Asia-Pacific region, they are rolling out their model in partnership with

AIA, and in Japan with Sumitomo. They have a minority equity stake in Ping An Health, allowing them to work closely with one of China's largest insurers. They have partnerships with companies such as John Hancock in the USA, Manulife in Canada, and Generali in Europe as well. Using this innovative partnership strategy, the South African start-up has grown quickly into a respected global player, with a market cap of over $8 billion and a foothold in many major markets internationally. According to founder Adrian Gore, one of the key sources of innovative energy for Discovery Group is that rewards and risk-taking go hand in hand. Each manager's performance evaluation includes an innovation score. The company also holds a lucrative annual competition to identify creative new ideas. These and other organizational efforts help to maintain its signature focus on innovation as the company continues to grow and mature.

Sources: https://www.discovery.co.za/portal/; https://www.mckinsey.com/industries/healthcare-systems-and-services/our-insights/how-discovery-keeps-innovating; https://store.hbr.org/product/discovery-limited/715423?sku=715423-PDF-ENG

BE AN ENTREPRENEUR

Regardless of whether leaders are actual founders of their organizations or not, innovation requires leaders to retain an entrepreneurial streak. This entails multiple factors, including being creative, being willing to experiment and take risks, and learning from both failures and customer insights. To accomplish this, it is important that leaders attain top management support, remain flexible in the face of change, and keep close tabs on consumer preferences.

Start Innovation at the Top

Our research revealed that one of the most critical factors of leading for innovation is that there must be clear and vocal support for innovation at the very highest levels of the organization. Although innovation has been a chief concern for CEOs for some time, the COVID-19 pandemic has made this even more of a formalized priority. According to Ramon Baeza, GM and Senior Partner of Boston Consulting Group and an author of the BCG Most Innovative Companies 2021 Report,[1] the share of companies reporting innovation as a top-three priority has jumped ten full percentage points to 75% from 2020 to 2021. In addition, the report shows that among the world's most innovative companies (measured by sales from new products and services) nearly 90% reported clear C-suite-level ownership of this priority whereas only 20% of innovation laggards reported the same. Innovation must not only be communicated as a clear strategic priority, but there must be resources attached to help make this vision become a reality.

Jun Wang, the country president of Oerlikon China, suggested that top managers should be bold enough to decisively choose to focus on innovation. At the same time, however, he recognized the importance of being able to convince the team that this is the right strategy through constant communication (rather than just forcing people to execute via the chain of command). Once the leader clearly communicates the priority and builds trust with the stakeholders, they will be on board even for projects that take a long time to bear fruit. He shared that

> stakeholders will back you up even when they cannot see the outcomes yet. Therefore, I believe the most important thing as a leader is the influence you have on people.

Zhenping Zheng, the person responsible for building the Shanghai branch of the Openex Intelligent Technology firm, described in more detail the role that top managers play in establishing the innovation infrastructure. He believes his primary contributions as a leader are

> the selection of the teams, the determination of the direction, and the establishment of the corporate culture and the main system of the Shanghai branch. This is an open and changing process, however. I didn't want to fix it,

because all here are innovations that take place every day.
I would rather let it grow wildly at the beginning, then
summarize and make rules after some time.

In this way, he believes that managers must communicate
through their words and rewards that innovation is a priority but
avoid rigid rules in place so that the system can respond agilely to
changes.

Kern Peng, a Lab Head at Intel in the USA, agreed that top managers must first create and maintain the right systems, establish the
right cultural values, and empower talented people to learn and
try new things. Ramon from BCG also agreed that true innovation
must rely on active engagement within the organization's top leadership team. He contended that:

There are other factors that the CEO has to lead. First,
business model innovation, which is very important.
Second, the customer insight, then the digital transforma-
tion. Business model innovation means changing the value
proposition and the operating model of the company and
hence needs to be owned by the CEO. This can take the
form of a running a test of the current business model
and scanning for opportunities both inside and outside
the company.

The BCG Most Innovative Companies 2021 Report highlights
five priorities that top managers often struggle with as they attempt
to embed innovation in their companies. Ramon from BCG mentioned that it includes business model innovation, particularly
in response to disruptions, capturing deeper customer insights,
embracing capabilities that enable innovation and fast change, scaling digital capabilities, and leveraging venturing vehicles to complement the innovation in the core organization. With regard to
innovative capabilities, Ramon believes that top managers should
ensure that their organizations are engaging in an iterative cycle of
innovation (dubbed the "innovation flywheel"). This entails capturing user data to better understand customers and generating
insights from this that help them to design small-scale experiments

that, if successful, can be scaled-up in the form of innovative new products, services, and experiences for the end user. Thus, Ramon added that it is the CEOs responsibility to champion and elevate innovation to a user process, and to ensure that there are processes in place so that the company can disruptively pivot in response to new customer insights. As a final thought, he emphasized the importance of corporate venture projects, urging that:

> Company innovation cannot be based only in the R&D department. When it comes to creating impact from corporate CEOs, we need to make sure that they define a clear mandate for the corporate venture firm. Secondly, they need to recognize that their main budget allocation for each of these vehicles is part of the overall innovation. Finally, they need to ensure these projects are adding to the strategic competitive advantage of the parent company. You don't do corporate venture just because it's fun.

Other interviewees we spoke to emphasized that it is important that top managers have passion and a long-term vision, particularly if they are the founders of the organization. The anonymous executive of the Chinese electric carmaker NIO, also spoke about the imaginative ideas of the company's founder and the fact that he was willing to take many risks (even with his own money) to make the company successful. She shared that:

> In retrospect, you must admit that many of his decisions were far-sighted, even if there may be a lot of financial pressure in the short term. One of my biggest impressions at NIO is the difference between an entrepreneur and a professional manager. A professional manager may focus on returns, but an entrepreneur doesn't. An entrepreneur only wants to start a business.

The founder's passionate style of communicating and genuine belief in the success of his product helped him to earn the trust of investors that helped to get him through difficult financial times. As true disruptive innovation requires time, this leadership characteristic can be essential. The founder's ability to surround himself with talented people who have complementary strengths and novel perspectives are also critical. Leaders should not only encourage people to look at problems in different ways and consider new solutions, but they should also test the feasibility of innovative ideas by openly discussing the pros and cons with people who have different points of view. The NIO founder's eloquent communication style, passion, creativity, and open-mindedness have become infused into the company's culture over time. This was achieved by constantly discussing the organization's values and instilling these into the quarterly performance assessments. Though the process took time, eventually these values and priorities took hold.

INNOVATION STORIES

Taking Risks at the Top to Drive Innovation at NIO

NIO is a new Chinese electric car manufacturer that has revolutionized the industry with its innovative approach. One of its biggest innovations is the battery replacement program that helps customers avoid long hours charging their batteries by providing them with a fully charged replacement battery within five minutes.

The program faced a lot of obstacles when it was first put into place. All the government's policies were against battery replacement. The regulators didn't understand battery replacement, and the whole world didn't understand it. For the company to be in charge of changing the battery, the battery must be rented rather than owned along with the rest of the car. Thus, this was a legal barrier that needed to be resolved. Second, if the battery mode was rental, since the vehicle and the battery cannot be separated, if the whole car was purchased, there were many obstacles to rent the battery. The third obstacle was that if the car owners want a new battery, the company must collect the rent, and car owner wouldn't want to pay a high price.

> The battery cost was over 100,000 yuan. Who would bear this cost? NIO was not a big car company with a big cash flow at the time. The cash flow was still a problem even for normal vehicle sales. Batteries are non-standard assets. No financial institution was willing to help. Finally, the founder decided to do it despite all the obstacles. He said that this was what he had to do and that it could not be changed. Today, after experiencing so many ups and downs, it seemed to be the best decision.

Be Flexible in the Face of Change and Failure

Another key aspect of leading for innovation in an entrepreneurial way is being open to both change and failure. Changjun Sun, a Consultant for TÜV Rheinland in China, noted that leaders must have a healthy appetite for taking risks to take on innovative new projects. Similarly, one General Manager we interviewed noted that he allows employees to make mistakes in the pursuit of innovation and that he has earmarked roughly 3 million renminbi [HM1] for innovative failures, telling his employees that "I allow you to fail, but you must tell me why you fail, and you must constantly communicate with me." He also assured employees that, if they got his approval and constantly communicated with him through the implementation process, he would take responsibility for any of their failures along the way. If their innovation attempts are not communicated ahead of time, however, employees are asked to shoulder the full responsibility. He shared the example of an exchange with an employee that helped to strengthen open communication and underscore that certain mistakes can be tolerated:

> We recently had and issue where our packages were becoming deformed during transportation, leading many customers to return the goods. Over time, these returns caused huge losses to our company. I told the manager to be responsible for this. I asked him, why did he change

the packaging? He said that changing the packaging could save 30 cents for each set. I first praised him and said your intention of saving money is good and no problem. But, I said, what I want to criticize is that you have to take responsibility for this failure of your small innovation because you didn't communicate with your leader. As long as you report your suggested changes ahead of time, we will share the responsibility for this failure. In this way, I strengthened their communication norms, and eventually everyone in this company was actively communicating with their leaders.

Yang Bing, the Founder of DEWU, also believes that open communication is the key to ensuring that both employees and the organization at large can learn from failure. He shared that he allows employees the latitude to try new things as long as they don't have an enormous financial, legal, or reputational impact. He pairs this empowerment with feedback to ensure that lessons are learned from each project, regardless of whether it turns out to be a success or failure. Summarizing this approach, he shared that "through constant feedback (both positive and negative) employees can have a deeper and deeper understanding of things." Kenneth Yu, the former President of 3M Greater China Area, also believes in the importance of using failure as a developmental experience for employees and the company, sharing that

leadership has to treat failures as investment for success tomorrow. Failures never give you a net zero. In failures, we learn. In the culture of innovation, people are curious and entrepreneurial.

He also notes that diverse projects should be encouraged and not discarded even if they are initially unsuccessful because they may be simply ahead of their time. When people are encouraged to experiment and talk about their projects, others may be inspired to apply innovations in different contexts that might be more successful.

Our interviewees also remarked that innovation flourishes when employees on the frontline feel free to communicate directly with top managers. For example, at DEWU, employees are encouraged to speak directly with the founder, Yang Bing, when they have new ideas. Emphasizing the egalitarian nature of the organization, he shared that the employees don't call him Mr Yang, but rather just by his first name. He also noted that "in our company, we don't use any titles. I have no office. Any person can see me and find me or contact me through our messaging application." Kenneth from 3M shared that even in hierarchical cultures like China, people adapt very quickly to company norms that allow for this degree of open communication. The important factor is that leaders should not only have their doors and offices physically open, but that they proactively engage in conversations with people at all levels of the company. He noted that

> *in other organizations, they tell you follow the chain of command, and then somebody in the chain of command will kill the idea. In 3M, nobody would dare to kill an idea. If someone stops an idea from reaching the CEO, it is considered a sin.*

He also adopted this philosophy into his own leadership style, sharing that:

> *At 3M China, they don't call me Mr. Yu. They call me Big Brother. Even new people don't think of me as some-one who cannot be reached. If you have something very interesting, you can tell me. I actually wish I had more people who wanted to knock on my door to come to see me. Meeting people at the worker level is important. In Chinese, there's a saying about 'being where the tea touches the ground.' In English it's 'being where the rub-ber meets the road.' At the end of the day, you have to practice what you preach, because you help to create the atmosphere as the head of the company.*

As a final word, David Ferreira from Discovery underscored that leaders should be

*much more open in general to ideas from the outside,
much more open to ideas from the front line and from the
troop level, and much more influenced by people's knowledge than by their position in the organization.*

Use Customers to Drive Innovation

Echoing previous chapters, some respondents believed that global innovation efforts can learn from China's iterative approach.
Zhifeng Zhang, the Managing Director for Hotelbeds in Shanghai
believes that global companies should adopt more quick prototyping and adopt "the spirit of trial and error. It is relatively shortsighted to see an immediate return when doing something new." In
general, innovation leaders agreed that one of the most important
factors is for leaders to be proactive in gathering customer data
and responding to these insights. Ramon from BCG advocated
that companies should create a self-sustaining cycle of innovation
that features:

> *An iterative, customer centric, agile innovation process
> that is centered around the customer. Learning from every
> customer interaction is what we call the innovation fly-
> wheel. It implies major changes in a company's way of
> working, from its organizational design to its culture, to its
> leadership model. At the end of the day, it often amounts
> to significant transformation.*

Similarly, Changjun from TÜV Rheinland shared examples of how
empowering employees to pay close attention to customer needs
can result in big opportunities in innovative ways:

> *It is imperative for the salespeople to be creative, and we
> should help them understand the importance of being
> open to new things. I told the sales staff here to be mind-
> ful of the new requirements of our customers and give me
> feedback on their new requirements. For instance, once
> the Zimbabwe authorities required all importers to meet
> a certain standard, but the inspection standard was not
> available anywhere in Zimbabwe. Our salesman told me*

as soon as he got the call. I looked at it and found it quite a simple matter. I asked the client to describe their required standard, then our technical personnel quickly developed a whole series. As a result, a 10,000 yuan project became a 300,000 yuan project. A similar instance happened when we launched the new service of factory inspection and verification to the Alibaba e-business platform. Through adjusting original practices, the project grew, and the highest revenue reached over 35 million yuan.

This customer centricity also translates into clear goals and a shared passion for employees. By having all employees aligned under the mission of providing customers the most sustainable transportation option in the world and empowering those closest to the problems to solve them, employees are inspired to find novel ways to meet customer needs.

BE AN ORGANIZATIONAL SERVANT

Innovation also requires that leaders adopt a highly supportive attitude toward their followers. Building on the practice of empowerment, our research revealed that a second critical component of leading for innovation is engaging in servant leadership.[2] Servant leadership begins with the philosophy that the employees are the most important people in the organization, and that the leader's mission is first and foremost to serve and uplift them while helping them to become energized by the company's mission. These leaders also have strong visions, are aware of both their strengths and weaknesses, and remain humble. The most important aspects of being a true servant leader are breaking down hierarchies and empowering your team.

Let Go of Hierarchy and Authority

Our interviewees had different ways of describing this unselfish and non-authoritarian style of leadership. As an example, Yang from DEWU observed that:

> CEOs can make mistakes, they are usually not blamed in
> the company. But I think many CEOs are selfish and don't
> give the same opportunities to colleagues within a certain
> range. All our colleagues should be given the opportunity
> to make mistakes.

Kenneth from 3M shared that the leaders must commit – in terms of time, money, and resources – to supporting the innovation efforts of employees. In this way, the leader's role is to be patient enough and to provide the necessary ingredients for employees to succeed. Huijie Hong, the founder of MITS Technology, agreed that

> the most crucial thing is persistence. Drawing from my
> own experience, you must communicate your blueprint,
> your goal, and your determination with your team. These
> three are the keystones to success, and you must not
> change them when there are doubts. You can make adjust-
> ments or try new tactics without changing your keystones.

Jason Yin shared Kimberly-Clark China adopts a distinctly non-hierarchical and hands-on style of leadership in their day-to-day approach, noting that

> so many initiatives failed halfway because of the manage-
> ment style of that country's branch. If there is a hierar-
> chy or if the leadership isn't easy to approach, innovation
> can't be done.

Jason oversees the finances, but he also frequently helps make decisions about sales and marketing issues. Each of the different functional managers are aligned under the idea that research and development is a top priority given that having innovative new products is the key to growth. To instill this focus, the leadership organizes a quarterly innovation meeting where the market-ing, research, engineering, supply chain, operations, purchasing, and finance people meet to discuss new business opportunities. This all-hands meeting helps to avoid issues of misalignment and facilitates open communication and idea exchange among the different departments. Without such an initiative, Jason opined that:

*Each of the functions would still work separately. They
would have their own KPIs and interests. The solution is
very simple, that is, summoning all relevant stakeholders
to this innovation meeting. Everyone clarifies the problems, sets deadlines, and figures out obstacles. In that way,
our shared priority is very clear. Such coordination inte-
grates all resources to support the task, and then innovation can be achieved quickly. In innovation meetings, the
hierarchy is broken, and the leadership is there to help
everyone solve the problems. Therefore, the presentation
is often made by the people who are directly on the front
line. Everyone's passion for innovation is ignited.*

Although empowerment and servant leadership are important,
it is also critical to acknowledge that leaders focused on innovation still need to make tough decisions from time to time. Jari
Grosse-Ruyken, a Managing Partner at the Shanghai-based consulting group hivetime, shared that many of the best leaders he
has witnessed "were actually coaching their subordinates. They
were not saying "do this, do that," but rather they acted like an
ideal parent: coaching, guiding the subordinates through asking
smart questions." Still, he sees value in combining this style with
firm accountability and holding people responsible for meeting targets. Hang Li agrees that leaders must be willing to make tough
decisions to be truly innovative. He believes that leaders who are
focused on innovation must be flexible and able to accommodate
trial and error, but that decisions should also be dictated by objective data. As an example of this, he opined that

*when they try to seize an opportunity, they need to imme-
diately recruit a team. They will keep the team if it works.
But if it doesn't, they will not hesitate to dismiss the team.
Their way of thinking is tinged with wolf nature.*

Empower Your Team

With the top management team preoccupied by passionately communicating the importance of innovation, embodying cultural

values, and setting up the systems to react quickly to changing customer insights, innovative organizations require high levels of empowerment. Managers and lower-level employees must be able to make decisions that allow them to quickly respond to changes and leverage their localized insights. Summarizing this innovation enabler, Zhifeng Zhang, the Managing Director of Hotelbeds. com in Shanghai, believes that "global companies should do fewer things. They should try to empower and trust as much as possible. With independent resources, independent teams, and direct decision-making power, you may succeed." As an example of this approach, Jerry Liu, the President of Cargill China, noted that his boss would never give him detailed instructions of how to meet his targets. He shared:

> *My boss would never tell me, Jerry, you should do a head-count reduction. What he would tell me is to follow the consumer trends and grow your business, but it is up to the leaders to decide exactly what to do because they believe we are much closer to the ground, to the consumer, and we know exactly what they want. Our boss gives us areas that we want to go to grow. We have to find out how to do it.*

This soft-touch management style allows the individual units not only to be more flexible, but to also be more creative and diverse in how they meet the needs of their own local consumers. Thus, although there is a larger company-wide imperative at Cargill to be innovative and follow the trends of sustainability, vegetable-based foods, and health consciousness, the individual business units have a large degree of latitude to determine which products and business model innovations will meet their growth and innovation goals in a given market.

A Product Manager at a Chinese internet company shared that her organization also leverages empowering talent management tactics to maintain sustainable innovation efforts. This involves a high level of equality where diverse employees are expected to contribute their thoughts and objections during meetings. To ensure that people are moving in the right direction, top managers should celebrate people who have great ideas, high-levels of performance, and those who embody the company's innovation values. The Product Manager we spoke with shared that it is a good idea for managers

> to showcase what is good and bad, through which we can identify and promote certain events or people and make them role models for others. If I ever find out about a certain case that deserves a reward, I will promote these activities by issuing on-the-spot bonuses or some other prizes on a two-month basis in a public setting.

Finally, they believe that innovation should be continuously discussed between senior managers and lower-level employees and that people should always be encouraged to bring ideas forward about how the business can be adjusted.

Many of the entrepreneurs we spoke to were particularly keen on taking the empowerment of employees to the extreme. Cheng Hang, the founder of HUPU, believes in empowering people even to the point of helping his employees to start their own business ventures. He told us that he not only allows them to pursue their own ideas, but he also gives them seed funds and allows them to decide what company share structure that they want to set up. Similarly, Congwei Huang, the founder of Z-trip, shared that:

> The best way to lead innovation is by doing nothing. In the process of innovation, the top decision-maker who owns the right to make decisions should interfere with the team's innovation as little as possible. By doing this, the team members may put forward different ideas and make products through certain mechanisms, which is the most efficient way for operating companies, especially Internet companies. If all businesses are decided by the top decision-maker, or all the ideas come from him, I don't think such a company is promising.

INNOVATION STORIES

Letting Your Team Surprise You at HUPU by Hang Chen

Pretty much every year the company and the team has surprised me. I never dreamed of anything like what we have today. I have seen some of my friends, other entrepreneurs, they can project their company's trajectory 10 years from now, and I really envy that. I admire that. But I don't have the capability of doing that. Once I realized that I lack that kind of ability about five or six years ago, I started to think, what if I just gave up trying, admit that I don't have it and just let it go? Then I realized my partners and my executives, once I start to minimize my influence in the company, then their brains opened and their ideas started to come out. It was a fascinating experience for me.

Sometimes when we discussed about how this project should go or where the company should be in three years, I found that if I stop talking, other people start talking and brilliant ideas started coming out. I was amazed that a lot of their ideas were much better than mine. It came to a point that some of my partners actually told me during the years "this company is not what we ourselves want to do most. We all have a different idea. What if we part ways? What is the best way forward?"

There was a lot of a struggle, lots of tensions, as you can imagine, long-time partners who were parting ways. But once I accepted that as CEO, I adopted more of a supporting role in their entrepreneur career. Something different happened. Actually, my company is called HUPU Holding because we have around a dozen different companies running very different businesses right now. We have the original sports media company, we have an e-commerce company called Poison, we have a sports company which is the largest a basketball league in Douing (one of the two largest short video platforms in China). We also have a VC fund, and we have our own apparel brand. All these businesses are owned by their founders.

It started roughly five or six years ago. There were two triggers. The first one, as I told you, was when I realized and admitted to myself that I just didn't have the kind of ability to imagine a big future for everybody. The second trigger was our company was trying to launch an IPO in China and it didn't go well for all sorts of reasons. We stopped the IPO process. This made everybody disappointed, definitely people were down at that time, and we started to think about how we could bounce back from that and keep the morale high. Too many different ideas came up. I didn't pick just one idea. I just let everybody go with their own ideas. Many projects failed, but some of them were successful. One of those new companies was Poizon, founded by Yang Bing, my original partner at HUPU.

CONCLUSION

In this chapter we highlight the two main characteristics of innovative leaders: they should be both a servant and an entrepreneur. In practice, this means that leaders should both work dutifully to meet the needs of their employees and customers while also thinking in novel and unconstrained ways. This allows them to both capitalize off their own innovative ideas while empowering the ideas that employees extract directly from their interactions with customers. Innovative leaders must ensure that they are consistently setting a clear example and clearly communicating that innovation is a central priority for the company. They must also ensure that the organizational structure, policies, and resources are in place so that followers can act on their own innovative ideas and projects. By viewing themselves as mere servants in pursuit of a greater mission, leaders will be more inclined to listen to the ideas of others, will not punish well-intentioned mistakes, and will act on objective customer data and feedback even when it is surprising or goes against tradition.

ACTION POINTS LEADING FOR INNOVATION

Be an Entrepreneur

Start Innovation at the Top

Leaders play an integral role instilling a focus on innovation throughout every layer of the organization. Be clear and vocal in your support of innovation. Innovation must be core part of the strategy and resources must be available for employees to help them pursue these goals. Top management must show passion and have a long-term vision. Surround yourself with team members who have different perspectives that complement your own.

Be Flexible in the Face of Change and Failure
Allow people to fail within limits. Let them try new things as long they do not have an enormous financial, legal, or reputational impact. Ensure lessons are learnt from each project, regardless of whether it turns out to be a success or failure. Treat failures as investment for success tomorrow. Engage in conversations with people at all levels of the company.

Use Customers to Drive Innovation
Be proactive in gathering customer data and responding to these insights. Customers can be a great source of innovation.

Be a Servant

Let Go of Hierarchy and Authority
Make you main role to serve member of your organization and facilitate their work. Organize regular meetings with different areas in the organization to discuss new business opportunities. Coach your team, guide them, ask smart questions and hold them responsible for meeting targets.

Empower Your Team
Allow your managers and lower-level staff to make decisions so they can quickly respond to changes and leverage their localized insights. Promote open discussions in meetings regardless of the hierarchical level. Preach with your example. Celebrate and recognize people with great ideas and embody a culture of innovation.

NOTES

1. https://www.bcg.com/en-us/publications/2021/
most-innovative-companies-overview

2. https://www.shrm.org/resourcesandtools/hr-topics/organizational-and-employee-development/pages/the-art-of-servant-leadership.aspx

9

TRANSFORMATION TO BECOMING INNOVATIVE TO THE CORE

In the long run, the organizations which are agile, which can adapt faster to the change, and are innovative, are going to be the front runners.

– Kamal Dhuper, CEO of NIIT China

INTRODUCTION

After dissecting the components of what differentiates innovative countries, companies, and cultures, many readers may be wondering how they might embark on a change effort to implement some of these features in their own firms. In this chapter, we will focus on the process of this transformation. Finally, we will explore critical roles of the CEO leading the transformation. Namely, he or she must act as role model, architect, and the ultimate owner of the change process.

THE INNOVATION TO THE CORE TRANSFORMATION PROCESS

Every transformation process must address four questions: WHO, WHY, WHAT, and HOW. The "WHO" is the leader of the organization. He or she must initiate the transformation process, navigate through it, and sustain it into the future so the organization does not relapse back into old habits. At a fundamental level, the organization leader must answer the three other questions as represented in Fig. 9.1.

WHO: THE TRANFORMATION LEADER

One common theme in our conversations with innovation experts is that the transformation process must start at the top with the CEO driving and reinforcing this process. In doing so, the CEO

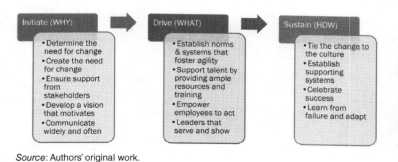

Source: Authors' original work.

Fig. 9.1. Innovation Transformation Process.

will serve three distinct functions. First, they should serve as role models. The CEO's words and actions must convincingly communicate the need for change and inspire hope for a better future. Second, they must act as the organizational architect. The CEO must introduce the necessary changes to the systems and policies of the organization, so that these act as the skeleton to support the flesh of the new innovative culture. As Kenneth Yu, the former CEO of 3M Greater China Area told us, innovation cultures cannot depend on a single person, but instead must be entrenched in the way things are done by everyone. The right systems create the conditions for innovation to happen independently of the person at the top, while also signaling what types of people are a good fit for top management positions in the future. Third, the CEO should be the change owner. He or she is the person ultimately responsible for the successful execution of the change. This requires perseverance, determination, and delegation to key support staff (Fig. 9.2).

This three-pronged role of the CEO during the change process is underscored by evidence from recent reports. For example, Ramon Baeza, Senior Partner at Boston Consulting Group and a co-author of the BCG Most Innovative Companies 2021 report highlighted that it is the CEO's job to bring various stakeholders together under a single future vision. As an example, he noted that 31% of respondents to their survey reported that poor collaboration between marketing and R&D was the biggest obstacle for a better return on innovation-related investments. To overcome this, they suggested that top management needs to create a one-team

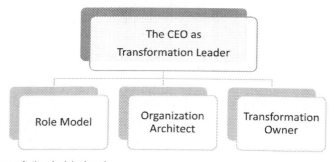

Source: Authors' original work.

Fig. 9.2. Three Roles of the CEO as the Transformation Leader.

mentality (i.e., act as a role model), align incentives with matching metrics and establish clear lines of communication, goals, and accountability (i.e., serve as the organization architect), and challenge the status quo while being sure to celebrate successes along the way (i.e., be a change owner).

The ultimate objective of this transformation is to achieve an organizational culture that features three core characteristics:

- *Psychological safety*: an organization where experimentation and learning are welcome.

- *Openness*: low power distance among different levels in the organization so ideas flow freely.

- *Diversity*: employees have diverse professional backgrounds, ages, genders, and nationalities.

The Transformation Advisory Board (referred to as the "TAB" from now on) can play a supporting role during this transformation process. We will cover the TAB as part of the HOW.

The CEO as a Role Model

Given that CEOs are at the top of the organization and are often quite visible to others, employees lower in the organization look to their words and actions to decipher what goals should be prioritized. Because of this, it is very important that CEOs use their platform to help employees understand what they stand to lose if things don't change and to paint a picture of how things might improve following the transformation. Creating a collective sense of urgency can sometimes be particularly difficult to do during times of success. This is because middle managers can get bogged down in a short-term orientation of maximizing quarterly goals and forget to lay the groundwork for long-term success. CEOs can re-focus the organization on long-term success by leveraging effective communication tools. The exact message may differ depending on the size and circumstances of the organization. For example, family-owned businesses or mid-sized companies in more collectivistic cultures may choose messages that center on tradition and the long-term imperative to secure a legacy.

In contrast, larger companies may use emotional speeches to demonstrate why becoming leaner or more agile helps to create more meaningful jobs and helps the company become more sustainable. As an example of such a transformation, Jari Gross-Ruyken, the German Managing Partner at hivetime, recounted the example of Volkswagen to us. This company was mired in scandal following "dieselgate" and top managers knew they could no longer turn a blind eye. Jari believes that the CEO, Mr Herbert Diess, used this crisis as an opportunity to create a sense of urgency for change. Today, Volkswagen has communicated that they will attempt to change their direction and embrace mobility by hiring thousands of coders and digital workers in Germany.

In addition to creating an impetus for change, the leader's words and actions should serve to unite the company under a single goal and mindset. Doing so will help to break up organizational silos and ensure that everyone is focused on the universal goal of, for example, meeting customer needs. One way to do this is to create a series of project teams or task forces that unite members from across the organization. Ramon from BCG observed that "cross-functional teams are a hallmark of many innovation leaders."

Another way to create uniform goals and expectations across all stakeholders is to ensure that the CEO can communicate clearly with both their organization and the market. By clearly explicating the link between innovation investments and future returns, everyone will be on board with spending the time and resources that are needed to drive long-term innovation. Finally, Ramon suggests that organizations should not rely on traditional ways of organizing their businesses. As an example, he opined that

> *companies should bring the top R&D, engineering, and business teams closer to the innovation agenda. In the past they were working on their own. By bringing them closer to the innovation agenda, R&D teams craft much more novel solutions to meet the customer's needs.*

After agreeing upon unified goals, top executives should engage in teambuilding meetings that allow them to build bonds and agree on how they will achieve common priorities.

The CEO as Organizational Architect

The first step in this effort is to identify where your organization currently is in terms of agility and innovation. Kamal Dhuper from NIIT, describes four primary types of organizations. The first are *reactive organizations*, which do not proactively monitor changes in their environment. When changes or threats do arise, they tend to be slow to react. *Adaptive organizations*, in contrast, do a better job of keeping tabs on their internal and external landscape. Because of this monitoring, they tend to be more agile and reactive to changes. The third type of organization is a siloed or *fragmented organization*. Because knowledge sharing is minimal between the various factions, these types of organizations react even more slowly than reactive organizations. Finally, *cohesive organizations* tend to fare better than fragmented organizations, but they are also generally not very flexible. Dhuper's firm conducted an Adaptive Learning Organization survey to determine the base rate of each type of organization, finding that 53% were either reactive or fragmented organizations, roughly 30% were cohesive organizations, and only 16% were innovative or adaptive organizations. This suggests that many firms could use the tips outlined in this chapter if they aspire to be truly agile and successful in today's dynamic world. Of note, Kamal believes that there are no cultural restrictions on who can become an innovative or adaptive organization. In our conversation with him, he mentioned that this framework

> *applies to any organization, whether it's Chinese, Japanese, American, or a global organization. It is a model about how you adapt. How can you be agile? How do you change? It doesn't matter what nationality an organization is. It's about the leadership of the organization, the people of the organization, and how they respond to change.*

The rest of the chapter addresses the question of how to become an innovative organization to the core.

In their role as organizational architect, it is also vital that the CEO carefully aligns incentives with the types of behaviors and values they are trying to reinforce among employees. Ramon from BCG believes that one key aspect of aligning incentives is to ensure that the "R&D and business teams introduce shared metrics that will help both the innovation function and the R&D function to collaborate more effectively." Group incentives can also help to ensure a unified mindset and foster cross-functional alignment, further breaking down organizational silos. Similarly, Jerry Liu from Cargill, suggested that organizations interested in promoting innovation should provide incentives not only for returns, but also for growth rates. In addition to incentives, Jari from hivetime suggests that the whole process of cultural change should be anchored on things that can be measured and that the team must be held accountable for bottom-line targets. He noted that

> you can be a visionary leader that comes up with a disruptive innovation and at the same time be really harsh and demand performance by a team. I don't see a contradiction there.

The CEO as a Transformation Owner

A final role that the CEO must play during the transition to a deeply innovative culture is that of change owner. This means that he or she must initiate the transformation process, devote the necessary time and resources to its success, and accept the responsibility for any missteps along the way. According to Ramon Baeza at BCG, the first step in this process is undergoing a thorough analysis of where the organization currently stands in terms of innovation and how ready the employees are to accept change. This process involves benchmarking not only against your peers and competitors, but also comparing your firm to the innovation happening in other industries and by the very top innovators in the world. Based on this, the CEO can then draft an innovation agenda, which is a type of road map and timeline for how the transformation will unfold. The most important factor at these early stages, he believes, is that:

The process of innovation should be owned by the CEO. That's more and more important at the execution stage. This also includes the board. [To succeed in this transformation], they should really have innovation as top priority and ensure that they allocate and assign resources, both economic and people, to this cause. Align incentives with the strategy and align the whole organization with innovation.

After the auditing the current levels of innovation and formulating a transformation plan, Kamal Dhuper from NIIT advises that the CEO must then drive a series of learning transformations. This involves systematically questioning how agile the firm is, how it uses flexible variable capacity, how it leverages digital ecosystems, and how it optimizes personalized learning delivery. As he sagely notes,

becoming adaptive is a journey. The time and investment that is required to become an adaptive learning organization varies based on the size of the business organization. It doesn't happen overnight.

As part of this process, CEOs must also be sure that they are proactively changing their systems, processes, structure, resource allocation, and partnerships to be more responsive to customer needs while also becoming more sensitive to the changes in the internal and external environment. Ultimately, however, Kamal believes that the most daunting challenge facing the CEO is changing the culture, "because, in a way, you are changing the mindset of the people."

One way that the CEO can help to communicate the need for this transformation is to highlight what the company – and employees – stand to lose if they do not make these changes. As Jari from hivetime observed,

let's be honest, people like to stay in their comfort zone. If business is going well, the likelihood that the top executive team of this organization undergo potentially painful changes, is very limited.

Often, Jari notes, finding the right catalyst for cultural change is akin to introducing the right species in a natural ecosystem. He shared the story of how wolves were reintroduced into the Yosemite National Park in California as an analogy.

They reintroduced wolves and the whole biosphere of the park changed. The wolves started a chain of changes. The wolves kept the deer away so plants could grow that were previously eaten away by them. This had an impact on the soil because of the plants. Now other animals were attracted. Just by introducing one animal, the whole ecosystem changed. And what we try to do in organizations is we try to identify the wolf. What will be the wolf that ignites this domino effect of change?

The General Manager of a private company that preferred to remain anonymous also highlighted that the biggest barrier he faced while implementing a new innovative strategy was the ability and motivation of employees to go along with this change. Because the company had been detached from the market and principles of modern management for many years, he first embarked on an education campaign to help his employees understand why change was necessary. To build their understanding, he had them read management books and held sessions where he interpreted what these principles meant in the context of their industry. From there, he began by empowering small teams of people who believed in the necessity of innovation to break down the larger innovation strategy into smaller and more manageable steps so that everyone understood what they should do. As the leader, the General Manager we spoke with then insured that the incentives and bonuses were aligned with the implementation of these innovative steps. At every stage of this transformation, he was consistently viewed as the driver of the innovation initiative.

During the early stages of innovation, I talked a lot. I had meetings with the managers of all departments repeatedly in public workplaces for the first several months. I would

also have a drink with them privately, inviting them to my
home, telling them stories, and letting them trust me. If
there would be any problems, I would take responsibility so
they would not be worried about it. Things like this, I kept
telling them all the time. It was quite energy consuming.

The importance of persistence was also highlighted by
Changjun Sun of TÜV. He noted that many of his peers rejected
some early innovative ideas about new operations and marketing techniques "just because it was something new. They felt it
impossible because it was out of their product range. It is just
a habitual thinking." This suggests that the CEO is ultimately
responsible for defending innovation efforts against all opposition and helping to put the policies, resources, and education
in place so that the transformation efforts have every chance of
succeeding.

WHY: INITIATE THE NEED FOR INNOVATION

The leader must convince the organizational stakeholders of the
need for innovation. He or she must develop clear arguments to
support the transformation. In doing so, it is important to make
sure there is ample support across the organization to support the
change. The main practices are:

- Determine the need for change.

- Ensure support from stakeholders.

- Create the need for change.

- Develop a vision that motivates.

- Communicate widely and often.

A final way that interviewees suggested that CEOs must a
vision to convey the importance of innovation in such a way that
it makes work more meaningful for all employees. A great example
of this comes from the Chinese electric vehicle maker, NIO. The

company's founder does a masterful job of communicating a vision that engages. He once told his employees:

> *In such an unpredictable era, science and technology are advancing every day, especially under the fierce competition for new energy vehicles. If there is no innovation, we won't survive. What he means is that as a new company, we do not have deep experience like Huawei or Xiaomi or Apple in software or Baidu in autonomous driving. We are a brand-new team that was founded in 2015 or 2016. If we don't innovate, we will fail quickly.*

To further sell employees on the importance of surviving, NIO's CEO connects the company's vision to the future of China as a whole and other important trends including 5G and the Internet of Things (IoT). In a particularly passionate appeal, he shared with employees that

> *if we do not innovate, we will really lose this opportunity. It may not only mean that NIO vehicles will lose this opportunity, but China has also lost an opportunity for the taking the lead in this sector, because the industrial chain it drives is too huge. Once the entire industrial chain is established, it will be much bigger than Apple's mobile phones and we may become bigger than Apple.*

It is clear to see how such a powerful and exciting future vision can unite employees to work hard to achieve this goal and how people may be motivated to put aside their individual concerns for this larger cause.

WHAT: DRIVE THE TRANSFORMATION

The leader should ensure that the organization incorporates all components of the "Innovative to the Core" model:

Although the model implies a certain hierarchy or order to the steps, all the rings must be implemented simultaneously. As we saw

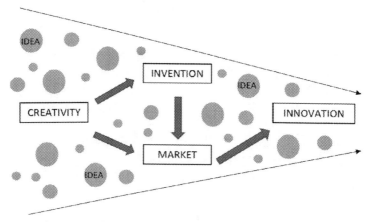

Source: Authors' original work.

Fig. 9.3.   The Funnel Model of Innovation.

in previous chapters, each of the elements entails specific behaviors as indicated in Table 9.1.

HOW: IMPLEMENT THE TRANSFORMATION

Leaders and team members must synchronize their efforts to ensure that the organization becomes innovative to the core. Some important actions at this stage include:

- Tie the change to the company culture.

- Establish supporting systems.

- Celebrate successes.

- Learn from failures and adapt.

Another important step in the implementation stage is the creation of a TAB to oversee the whole process.

Leverage the TAB

Although the CEO must play three integral roles when making the change to a deeply innovative organization, it does not mean that

Table 9.1 Components of Innovative Organizations.

Culture	Norms and Systems	Talent	Leadership
Create a culture that is innovative to the core:	*Become agile:*	*Talent for innovation:*	*Be entrepreneurial:*
Promote psychological safety	Break up organizational silos	Identify talent that fits with a culture of innovation	Be flexible in the face of change and failure
Foster openness	Be responsive to the external environment and make rapid decisions	Create an inviting environment that attracts desirable recruits	Use customers to drive innovation*Become a servant:*
Hire for diversity	Use your competition as an innovation impetus	Motivate them so they stay	Let go of hierarchy and authority
	Connect performance to KPIs and rewards		Empower your team
	Make innovation a core organizational value		
	Quickly approve and monitor innovation projects		
	Learn from failure and create trust		
	Make your processes more agile		
	Form partnerships for innovation		

Source: Authors' original work.

they are alone in this crusade. An important element for the success
of this cultural change is the creation of a TAB that reports directly
to the CEO. Jari from hivetime highlighted the importance that this
support team can play by noting that:

> There's a lot of talk about how top leader behavior is the
> key driver of change in organizational cultures. I strongly
> believe that. But it's very naive to just rely on the behavioral
> change of certain top executives. We all know that chal-
> lenge when we do our New Year's resolutions. "I want to
> lose weight. I want to exercise more. I want to read more."
> Usually, these efforts fail because we only rely on our will-
> power. We have limited willpower, and we need it for deal-
> ing with daily challenges in our work. After a couple of
> weeks, the New Year's resolution is all but forgotten. The
> same happens with culture change in organizations.

Often, organizations expect that Human Resources (HR) will
be the key driver of cultural change, which is a mistake. Although
they can serve in a support role as the people who orchestrate who
gets promoted, hired, and rewarded, there needs to be more buy-in
and more accountability for all the key functions at the top layer
of management. Otherwise, HR is often not given the resources or
authority to truly implement the change, and they end up becoming
the scapegoat for failure. Because of this, we recommend that HR
executives should be combined with other top managers to ensure
that all aspects of the business are aligned under the same innovation priority (Fig. 9.4).

The TAB's role is to support the CEO in the transformation
of the organization. The TAB includes executives and external
advisors depending on the transformation needs of the particular organization. The external members may be experts in certain
fields that provide advice but are not part of the decision processes.
The other members of the TAB are executives with enough power
and expertise to support the transformation effort. The main functions that must be represented are HR, Finance, and Operations.
If the company has business units, the head of those business units
are also part of the TAB. Other departments like IT can also be
represented depending on the exact types of innovation that the
company is hoping to pursue.

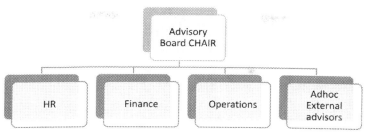

Source: Authors' original work.

Fig. 9.4.   Components of the TAB.

It is important that the members of the TAB have certain personal qualities. For example, they must be proactive, good networkers, critical thinkers, system thinkers, and empathetic. Moreover, they should have good knowledge of the company and the environment and have diverse background and thinking styles. The primary responsibilities of the TAB are to:

- Oversee and coordinate the transformation process.

- Support the middle managers.

- Evaluate requests from changes in the transformation process.

- Assign resources and people to the different initiatives.

- Measure results.

- Review and adapt plans.

Together with the CEO's support and guidance, a strong and unified TAB will ensure that the innovation priorities trickle down the organizational hierarchy and take root in the culture and norms of the organization.

CONCLUSION

When undertaking a cultural transformation to create an organization that is innovative to the core, it is critical that the CEO or Founder acts as the champion or driver of the change process. This involves tailoring your messages to emphasize innovation, making sure that the correct structures and policies are in place to foster innovation, and taking responsibility for any missteps or problems that occur during the transformation. He or she does not need to act alone, however. They should also create and leverage an expert cross-functional team of executives to serve on the TAB. These individuals will provide ideas and help to execute the change mandates at all levels of the organization.

ACTION POINTS

Who: The Tranformation Leader

The CEO as the Transformation Role Model
Employees at all levels look at the CEO's words and actions to decipher what goals should be prioritized. Leaders must unite the company under a single vision and mindset.

The CEO as an Organizational Architect
The CEO must be willing to continuously adapt their management methods, organizational structures, and technology to cope with the changing tides. Headquarters must give decision-autonomy to local teams so they can respond quickly to changes in the environment.

The CEO as the Transformation Owner
The CEO must initiate the transformation process, devote the necessary time and resources to its success, and accept the responsibility for any missteps along the way. He or she drafts the innovation agenda, including the road map and timeline for the transformation to unfold. The CEO should also empower small teams to translate the innovation strategy into smaller and more manageable steps. The CEO is ultimately responsible for defending the innovation efforts against all opposition and helping put the policies, resources, and education in place for the transformation to succeed.

Why: Initiate the Need for Innovation

Determine the need for change, ensure support from stakeholders, create the need for change, and develop a vision that motivates.

What: Drive the Transformation

Create a culture that is innovative to the core by becoming agile, hiring talent that fits, and having a leader that is entrepreneurial and acts as a servant to his team.

How: Implement the Transformation

Tie the change to the company culture, establish supporting systems, celebrate success, and learn from failure. Leverage the TAB and delegate the execution of the process to them. The TAB oversees and coordinates the process, review results, and adapts the agenda as needed.

10

CONCLUSION

Innovating is really fun; it is something that people want to do. I urge companies, corporations, schools, and universities to innovate because they will have a much brighter future and they will have much more motivated stakeholders.

– Ramon Baeza, Senior Partner at BCG

With this book, we have investigated why certain countries and companies are more innovative than others. On the macro level, we found that countries that have unique historical and cultural factors, those that prioritize high-quality education, those that emphasize national security and stability, and those that allow free movement across geographical clusters are the most innovative. We also found that innovation is not bound to country size, although this factor may determine the degree of specialization that a country chooses. We also highlighted several unique lessons that the world can learn from China's unique brand of innovation, including the importance of iterative improvements and experimentation. On the micro-level, our research determined that psychological safety, openness to new ideas, and diversity are the key pillars of an innovative culture. We also propose that deeply innovative cultures are both made up of and contribute to competent leadership (i.e., people who act as both servants and entrepreneurs), systems and policies that foster agility, and talent management that attracts and retains bright, ethical, diverse, and curious employees.

To conclude, we would like to take a moment to emphasize why it is so critical that the world learns to be innovative to the core at this moment in history. For one, the COVID-19 pandemic has clearly exposed many of the flaws in our previous ways of doing business and has revealed how ill-prepared many nations and companies were in responding to such dramatic changes. As the way we work continues to evolve going forward, it is important that we leverage the opportunity presented by this fresh start to implement the types of transformations that are needed to make us more agile and innovative. Over the course of our interviews, this innovation imperative was perhaps best summarized by Ramon Baeza, GM and Senior Partner at BCG:

> Innovation now is much more important than ever. As you can see from China, we are living in a world of disruption, disruption is becoming more and more important for every single business. No one can live with complacency. Many companies, successful companies, claim that they are doing fine. But when you are succeeding is the moment to change. Otherwise, it will be too late. Companies

should not get complacent, they should think about how to innovate, looking further into where to invest and how innovation is going to drive the future of their company. Innovation really is the driver for value creation, but I would say that also it's a way to motivate your company.

Even in pre-COVID times, there were several disruptive trends that required companies to be more creative and responsive. Especially in China, we see that new technologies and business models have completely upended a wide range of industries. As Kamal Dhuper, the CEO of NIIT China, shared with us,

you see a lot of innovation in China today. You see a lot of business model innovations in many industries. It could be in Fintech, it could be in EdTech, it could be in e-commerce. I think China is a hotbed for innovations. A lot of innovations that are happening in China are also starting to get replicated outside of China.

This point brings us to a final critical argument that we want to emphasize at the close of this book, and that is why China and the World need each other to succeed and have so much yet to learn from one another. For one, the world has become far too globalized and integrated to remain siloed off. Cameron Johnson, a Partner at Tidalwave Solutions, shared this insightful opinion in this regard:

There are two main processes today going on in the world today: integration and disintegration. We are integrating everything, integrating travel, technology, ourselves. We're intermarrying. We're doing all kinds of things that are integrating humanity that did not happen a century ago, or in some cases even 10 years ago. We are also seeing disintegration at the same time. The old ways of thinking, the old ways of doing things, old structures, societal institutions, and even governments, all of them are disintegrating and falling apart. What we're now looking for, and this is the real innovation part, are new ways of thinking and doing things that have never existed before. Not just tweaking a couple of processes, but true innovation.

How are we going to solve the world's problems? It's not by taxation, making everybody the same, or trying to improve the existing structures. Those two things have been tried and have proven unsuccessful in resolving the world's challenges. It's by thinking of new ways to integrate further, innovate further, and helping each other that are all critical components to fixing these problems. It's not easy, but this is the true innovation that humanity is going to have to create and go through.

Jonathan Woetzel, a Senior Partner at McKinsey, also shared similar concluding thoughts about China and the world:

China's relationship with the world is important, of course for both China and the world. While there are a lot of ways in which and it's important that China and Chinese companies compete in the world, it's also important to preserve areas in which there's opportunities for collaboration. There are probably four ways in which China and the world can continue to collaborate and to preserve what we might call a basis for ongoing engagement that are very important to both China and the world.

Of those four areas, the most obvious is technology, which is ultimately a global responsibility. There are many technological innovations that will never happen if we don't have an open relationship between China and the world. We need to scale technology and technology needs bigger markets. That will only happen if both China and the world are frequently cooperating and interacting with each other. Second, there's an important opportunity for China to continue to become more productive by introducing foreign investment in China. This goes both ways by also allowing Chinese companies to go abroad and invest. The world economy receives productivity benefits, and foreign investment raises the productivity of everything around it. Third, the simple fact that the Chinese economy will continue to grow and will become a bigger source of demand for the global economy. This increased demand provides more opportunities for exporters and for lower income countries in particular to develop their economies. Preserving openness around the trade of goods and services is a third way in which China and the world can win together. Lastly are the public goods like the environment or health, where it's very clear that China and the world need to maintain a basis for engagement. Without open lines of communication, we will lose the ability to defend the environment, to decarbonize it, and to ward off future pandemics. In sum, there are four ways that China and the world can win together: technology, foreign investment, demand, and public goods.

Of course, like any worthwhile transformation, this path to improved collaboration and innovation with be a struggle at times. We agree with Kamal from NIIT's assertion that this effort will ultimately prove to be fruitful:

It's a journey, but it's a journey which is definitely worthwhile taking because as we get into the next decade, there's going to be a lot of transformation, there's going to be a lot of change. You should aspire to become an adaptive organization which helps you stay relevant for a longer period of time.

INDEX

Printed in the United States
by Baker & Taylor Publisher Services